THE

OUTBREAK OF REBELLION

THE OUTBREAK

OF

REBELLION

BY

JOHN G. NICOLAY
PRIVATE SECRETARY TO PRESIDENT LINCOLN

CASTLE BOOKS

CAMPAIGNS OF THE CIVIL WAR.—I.
THE OUTBREAK OF REBELLION

This edition published in 2002 by Castle Books,
A division of Book Sales Inc.
114 Northfield Avenue, Edison, NJ 08837

First published in 1881.
Written by John G. Nicolay.

ISBN: 0-7858-1573-2

Printed in the United States of America.

PREFACE.

Upon urgent and repeated request from the publishers, the author consented to lay aside temporarily a larger and more important literary task, to write for them this initial volume of the "Campaigns of the Civil War." Personal observation and long previous investigation had furnished him a great variety of new material for the work; and this was opportunely supplemented by the recent publication of the Official War Records for 1861, both Union and Confederate, opening to comparison and use an immense mass of historical data, and furnishing the definite means of verifying or correcting the statements of previous writers.

Under these advantages the author has written the present volume, basing his work on materials of unquestioned authenticity—books, documents, and manuscripts—and, indeed, for the greater part, on official public records. His effort has been a conscientious and painstaking one, making historical accuracy his constant aim. If, unfortunately, he has committed any errors, he hopes they may prove only such as from the meagreness or conflicting nature of the evidence any one might fall into. He would gladly have appended to his pages full references and citations, but want of space absolutely forbade.

So many kind friends have encouraged and aided him, that he finds it impossible to acknowledge their services in detail, and therefore takes this occasion to return to one and all his sincere thanks. Government officials, especially, of all grades, have with uniform courtesy afforded him every facility in their power. Without free access to the various departments and archives—and, above all, to the vast historical treasures of the Library of Congress—it would have been exceedingly difficult to gather and verify the numerous facts, quotations, names, and dates, which his narrative required.

Washington, D.C.,
     February 26, 1881.

CONTENTS.

CONTENTS.

LIST OF MAPS.

THE OUTBREAK OF REBELLION.

CHAPTER I.

SECESSION.

THE fifth day of October, 1860, is the initial point of the American Rebellion. Its conception, animus, and probably its plans, lay much farther back. It had been seriously proposed once or twice before, but it was then that its formal organization was begun. On that day Governor Gist, of South Carolina, wrote a confidential circular letter, which he despatched by the hand of a special messenger, to the governors of what were commonly designated the Cotton States. In this letter he asked an interchange of opinions which he might be at liberty to submit to a consultation of leading men of South Carolina. He said South Carolina would unquestionably call a convention as soon as it was ascertained that a majority of Lincoln electors were chosen in the then pending presidential election. "If a single State secedes," he said, "she will follow her. If no other State takes the lead, South Carolina will secede (in my opinion) alone, if she has any assurance that she will be soon followed by another or other States; otherwise it is doubtful." He asked information, and advised concerted action.

North Carolina was first to respond. The people would

not, so wrote the governor under date of October 18th, consider Lincoln's election a sufficient cause for disunion, and
the Legislature would probably not call a convention.   The
Governor of Alabama, under date of October 25th, thought
Alabama would not secede alone, but would secede in co-
operation with two or more States.   The Governor of Mississippi, under date of October 26th, wrote: "If any State
moves, I think Mississippi will go with her."   On the same
day the Governor of Louisiana answered : "I shall not advise
the secession of my State, and I will add that I do not think
the people of Louisiana will ultimately decide in favor of
that course."   The Governor of Georgia, under date of October 31st, advocated retaliatory legislation, and ventured his
opinion that the people of Georgia would wait for some
overt act.   Florida alone responded with anything like enthusiasm, but only after the lapse of a month.   Her governor said that Florida was "ready to wheel into line with the
gallant Palmetto State, or any other Cotton State or States,"
and thought she would unquestionably call a convention.

The discouraging tone of these answers establishes, beyond
controversy, that, excepting in South Carolina, the rebellion
was not in any sense a popular revolution, but was a conspiracy among the prominent local office-holders and politi-
cians, which the people neither expected nor desired, and
which they were made eventually to justify and uphold by
the usual arts and expedients of conspiracy.

Directly and indirectly, the South had practically controlled the government during its whole existence.   Excited
to ambition by this success, she sought to perpetuate that
control.   The extension of slavery and the creation of additional Slave States was a necessary step in the scheme, and
became the well-defined single issue in the presidential election.   But in this contest the South for the first time met

overwhelming defeat. The choice of Lincoln was a conclusive and final decision, in legal form and by constitutional majorities, that slavery should not be extended; and the popular vote of 1860 transferred the balance of power irrevocably to the Free States.

In the political discussions throughout this presidential campaign, as well as in preceding years, the South had made free and loud use of two leading arguments, always with telling effect: the first, to intimidate the North, was the threat of disunion; the second, to "fire the Southern heart," was the entirely unfounded alarm-cry that the North, if successful, would not merely exclude slavery from federal territories, but would also destroy slavery in the Slave States. The unthinking masses of the South accepted both these arguments in their literal sense; and Southern public opinion, excited and suspicious, became congenial soil in which the intended revolt easily took root.

The State of South Carolina, in addition, had been little else than a school of treason for thirty years. She was, moreover, peculiarly adapted to become the hotbed of conspiracy by the fact that of all the States she was least republican in both the character of her people and the form of her institutions. She was exclusive, aristocratic, reactionary; had a narrow distrust of popular participation in government, and longed for the distinctions of caste and privilege in society.

It would seem that, before the governors' replies were all received, the consultation or caucus for which they were solicited was held, and the programme of insurrection agreed upon. Circumstances rendered a special session of the South Carolina Legislature necessary. The election was held during the month of October. Local fanaticism tolerated no opposition party in the State, and under the manipulation of the conspirators the prevailing question was, who was the most zealous "resistance" candidate. To a legislature elected from this kind of material, Governor Gist, on November 5th, sent a defiant, revolutionary message—the first official notice and proclamation of insurrection. He declared that "our institutions" were in danger from the hostility of the "fixed majorities" of the North; and recommended the calling of a State convention, and the purchase of arms and material of war.

A lingering doubt about the result of the presidential contest appears in the formal choice by the Legislature, of electors who would vote for Breckinridge and Lane. But that doubt was short-lived. The morning of November 7th brought the certain news of the election of Lincoln and Hamlin on the previous day, and the rejoicings which would have been uttered over their defeat became jubilations that their success offered the long-coveted pretext for disunion.

From this time forth everything was managed to swell the revolutionary furor. The Legislature immediately ordered a convention, made appropriations, passed military bills. The federal office-holders, with much public flourish of their patriotic sacrifice, resigned their offices. Military companies enrolled themselves in the city; organizations of minutemen sprang up in the rural neighborhoods. Drills, parades, meetings, bonfires, secession harangues, secession cockades, palmetto flags, purchase of fire-arms and powder, singing of the Marseillaise—there is not room to enumerate the follies to which the general populace, especially of Charleston, devoted their days and nights. There was universal satisfaction: to the conspirators, because their schemes were progressing; to the rabble, because it had a continuous holiday.

Amid unflagging excitement of this character, which received a daily stimulus from similar proceedings beginning and growing in other Cotton States, November and the first half of December passed away. Meanwhile a new governor, Francis W. Pickens, a revolutionist of a yet more radical type than his predecessor, was chosen by the Legislature and inaugurated, and the members of the Convention authorized by the Legislature were chosen at an election held on December 6th. The South Carolina Convention met at Columbia, the capital of the State, according to appointment, on December 17, 1860, but, on account of a local epidemic, at once adjourned to Charleston. That body was, like the Legislature, the immediate outgrowth of the current conspiracy, and doubtless counted many of the conspirators among its members. It therefore needed no time to make up its mind. On the fourth day of its term it passed unanimously what it called an Ordinance of Secession, in the following words:

"We, the people of the State of South Carolina, in convention assembled, do declare and ordain, and it is hereby declared and ordained, that the ordinance adopted by us in convention on the 23d day of May, in the year of our Lord 1788, whereby the Constitution of the United States of America was ratified, and also all Acts and parts of Acts of the General Assembly of this State ratifying amendments of the said Constitution, are hereby repealed; and that the Union now subsisting between South Carolina and other States, under the name of the United States of America, is hereby dissolved."

Conscious that this document bore upon its face the plain contradiction of their pretended authority, and its own palpable nullity both in technical form and essential principle, the convention undertook to give it strength and plausibility by an elaborate Declaration of Causes, adopted a few days later (December 24th)—a sort of half-parody of Jefferson's masterpiece. It could, of course, quote no direct warrant from the Constitution for secession, but sought to deduce one, by implication, from the language of the Declaration of Independence and the Xth Amendment. It reasserts the absurd paradox of State supremacy—persistently miscalled "State Rights"—which reverses the natural order of governmental existence; considers a State superior to the Union; makes a part greater than the whole; turns the pyramid of authority on its apex; plants the tree of liberty with its branches in the ground and its roots in the air. The fallacy has been a hundred times analyzed, exposed, and refuted; but the cheap dogmatism of demagogues and the automatic machinery of faction perpetually conjures it up anew to astonish the sucklings and terrify the dotards of politics. The notable point in the Declaration of Causes is, that its complaint over grievances past and present is against certain States, and for these remedy was of course logically barred by its own theory of State supremacy. On the other hand, all its allegations against the Union are concerning dangers to come, before which admission the moral justification of disunion falls to the ground. In rejecting the remedy of future elections for future wrongs, the conspiracy discarded the entire theory and principle of republican government.

One might suppose that this exhausted their counterfeit philosophy—but not yet. Greatly as they groaned at unfriendly State laws—seriously as they pretended to, fear damage or spoliation under future federal statutes, the burden of their anger rose at the sentiment and belief of the North. "All hope of remedy," says the manifesto, "is rendered vain by the fact that the public opinion at the North has invested a great political error with the sanctions of a more erroneous religious belief." This is language one might expect from the Pope of Rome; but, that an American convention should denounce the liberty of opinion, is not merely to recede from Jefferson to Louis XIV.; it is flying from the town-meeting to the Inquisition.

Nor can the final and persistent, but false assumption of the South, be admitted, that she was justified by prescriptive privilege; that, because slavery was tolerated at the formation of the government, it must needs be protected to perpetuity. The Constitution makes few features of our system perpetually obligatory. Almost everything is subject to amendment by three-fourths of the States. The New World Republic was established for reform—not for mere blind conservatism, certainly not for despotic reaction. The slavery question, especially, was ever since 1808 broadly under the control of the people. On the one hand, Congress had legal power to tolerate the African slave trade; on the other, three-fourths of the States might lawfully abolish slavery, as was done near the close of the Rebellion. To effect necessary and salutary political changes, in the fulness of time, by lawful and peaceful election through constitutional majorities, as a prudent alternative to the violence and horror of revolution, is one of the many signal blessings which republican representative government confers on an intelligent nation.

The Ordinance of Secession of South Carolina was passed in secret session, a little after mid-day, on December 20th. The fact was immediately made public by huge placards issued from the Charleston printing-offices; and by special direction of the convention, the event was further celebrated by firing guns, ringing bells, and other jubilations. To carry this studied theatrical effect to its fullest extent, a session of the convention was held that same night, to which the members marched in procession, where the formal signing of the Ordinance was sought to be magnified into a solemn public ceremony; after which the chairman proclaimed South Carolina an "independent commonwealth." With all their affectation of legality, formality, and present justification, some of the members were honest enough to acknowledge the true character of the event as the culmination of a chronic conspiracy, not a spontaneous revolution. "The secession of South Carolina," said one of the chief actors, "is not an event of a day. It is not anything produced by Mr. Lincoln's election, or by the non-execution of the Fugitive Slave Law. It is a matter which has been gathering head for thirty years." This, with many similar avowals, crowns and completes the otherwise abundant proof that the revolt was not only against right, but that it was without cause.

The original suggestion of Governor Gist in his circular letter, for a concerted insurrection, fell upon fruitful soil. The events which occurred in South Carolina were in substance duplicated in the neighboring States of Georgia, Florida, Alabama, Mississippi, and Louisiana. These States, however, had stronger and more formidable union minorities than South Carolina; or rather, if the truth could have been ascertained with safety, they had each of them decided majorities averse to secession, as was virtually acknowledged by their governors' replies to the Gist circular. But during the presidential campaign, the three Southern parties, for factional advantage, had vied with each other in their denunciations of the hated "Black Republicans"—they had berated each other as "submissionists" in secret league or sympathy with the Abolitionists. The partisans of Breckinridge—generally either active or latent disunionists—were ready, positive, and relentlessly aggressive; the adherents of Bell and of Douglas were demoralized and suspicious. When

Lincoln's election was, so unexpectedly to many, rendered certain, they could not recover in time to evade the searching question which the conspirators immediately thrust at them. "whether they would submit to Black Republican rule." A false shame and the inexorable tyranny of Southern public opinion made many a voter belie the honest convictions of his heart, and answer No, when at the very least he would gladly have evaded the inquiry.

The prominent office-holders, governors, senators, congressmen, judges, formed in each State a central clique of conspiracy. The governors had official authority to issue proclamations, to convene legislatures, to call out and command such militia as existed. Had their authority been wielded in behalf of the Union, no general revolt would have been possible ; but, exercised without scruple or rest to promote secession, insurrection began with an official prestige which swept the hesitating. and the timid irresistibly into the vortex of treason. Even then it was only by persistent nursing, management, and in many cases sheer deceit that a semblance of majorities was obtained to justify and apparently indorse the conspirators' plots. Legislatures were convened, commissioners sent from State to State, conventions called, military bills passed, minute-men and volunteer companies organized. Deliberative bodies were harangued by the conspirators' emissaries, and showered with inflammatory telegrams. After the meeting of Congress the fire-eaters of Washington held almost nightly caucuses, and sent addresses, solicitations, and commands from the capital. Individual opinion was overawed ; the government was not only silent, but constantly yielding ; legislative deliberation became, in secret session, legislative intrigue ; pretexts were invented to defer and omit all proper scrutiny of election returns. The "State" was the idol of the hour. "The State

1*

commands" was as despotic a formula as "The king commands"; and the voter's personal judgment, the very basis and life-giving principle of republics, was obliterated between the dread of proscription and the blighting mildew of the doctrine of supreme State allegiance.

Certain features of the struggle deserve special explanation. The "irrepressible conflict" between North and South, between freedom and slavery, was not confined to the two sides of Mason and Dixon's line; it found a certain expression even in the Cotton States themselves. Most of these States embrace territory of a radically different quality. Their southern and sea-coast front is a broad belt of sea-islands, marshes, river-swamps, and low alluvial lands, exceedingly unhealthy from malarial fevers in the hot season, but of unsurpassed fertility, and possessing the picturesque aspects of an exuberant half-tropical vegetation. This is the region of the great cotton, rice, and sugar plantations which have made the South rich and famous; here the St. Clairs and Legrees of real life counted their slaves by hundreds, and aspired to sybaritic lives in ample, hospitable mansions, surrounded by magnificent and venerable live-oak and magnolia groves, avenues of stately palms, princely gardens of native and exotic bloom, and illimitable hedge-lines of the Cherokee rose; a swarm of house-servants to minister to pampered indolence and dispense a lavish hospitality; a troop of field-hands to fill the cotton, rice, or sugar houses; a blending of Arcadian simplicity and feudal pretension; every plantation with its indulgent master, its exacting overseer, its submissive slaves. These were the lights of the picture; abler pens have painted the horrible background of bloody slave-whips, barbarous slave-codes, degrading slave-auctions, yellow fever, cypress-swamps, the bloodhound hunt, and the ever-present dread of servile insurrection. From such surroundings came the morbid dreams of an unholy league between perpetual bondage and free trade, which should rear a gigantic slave empire, before which the intellect, the power, the splendor, and the government of all preceding ages and nations should fade and wane.

The northern half of the Cotton States was very different; here were thin, sandy uplands of meagre productiveness; monotonous forests of pine and scrub-oak, running again into the more varied and romantic scenery of the subsiding spurs of the Alleghanies; blue crags, bright streams, shining waterfalls, and the changing, deciduous foliage of the North. Great slave-plantations could not flourish here; white population predominated; agriculture was varied; the husbandman had a sterner struggle with nature; and communities were burdened with all the economic and social detriments of the slave system, having none of its delights.

A dense slave population and ultra secessionism were, therefore, the rule in the southern, and white majorities and union feeling in the northern districts of the Cotton States. Therefore, also, political power lay in the slave region, which again was allied to the commercial interests clustering about southern seaports. All the leverage was in the hands of treason—offices, ostracism, advantage in representation, commercial ambition, party ascendancy. The wonder is, not that secession succeeded in the struggle, but that there was any serious contest at all. With all this, there is strong ground for belief that insurrection gained its ends at last only through chicane, deceit, and fraud. Not a single Cotton State but Texas dared to submit its Ordinance of Secession to a direct vote of the people.

The struggle assumed its most determined phase in Georgia. She was the Empire State of the South, and, therefore, indispensable to the conspiracy, in which distinguished citizens of hers—Governor Brown, Secretary Cobb, Senators Toombs and Iverson, and others—were conspicuous ring-leaders. The more rabid fire-eaters desired that the Legislature should at once pass an act of secession; Stephens and other conservatives opposed this course. "The Legislature were not elected for such a purpose," said he. "They came here to do their duty as legislators. They have sworn to support the Constitution of the United States. They did not come here to disrupt this government. I am, therefore, for submitting all these questions to a convention of the people." In due time a convention was called by unanimous vote of the Legislature. Then followed a spirited campaign to elect delegates. It early became evident that, while the people of Georgia were irritated to the point of demanding new guarantees for slavery, they were decidedly against disunion. Thereupon the conspirators invented a bold trick. "The truth is," explains Alexander H. Stephens, "in my judgment the wavering scale in Georgia was turned by a sentiment the key-note to which was given in the words, 'We can make better terms out of the Union than in it.' . . . . This one idea did more, in my opinion, in carrying the State out, than all the arguments and eloquence of all others combined. Two-thirds at least of those who voted for the Ordinance of Secession, did so, I have but little doubt, with a view to a more certain reformation of the Union." The heresy of supreme State allegiance was, however, the final and all-conquering engine of treason. Mr. Stephens him-self, in his memorable speech in defence of the Union, is the striking illustration of Gulliver helpless in the cobwebs of Lilliput. To secede, he declared, was to break the Constitution. Good faith required the South to abide the election in peace. Lincoln could do her no harm against an adverse House and Senate. He adjured them not to rashly try

the experiment of change; for liberty, once lost, might never
be restored. These were words of sober wisdom, and, fear-
lessly adhered to by a few firm men, they might have paralyzed the revolt. Yet in the same speech he declared that,
if Georgia seceded, he should bow to the will of her people
—in other words, break the Constitution, break faith, and
lose liberty. On this "easy descent" Georgia slid to her
ruin. Under such examples the convention passed the secession ordinance, 208 to 89.

While thus in the States of South Carolina, Georgia, Alabama, Florida, Mississippi, and Louisiana, the conspiracy
made pretentious efforts to clothe rebellion in the robes of
law, and hide it behind the shield of constitutional forms, it
pursued an altogether bold and unblushing course of usurpation in the State of Texas. The famous and somewhat
eccentric General Houston was governor. His own long
struggle to bring Texas into the Union made him loth to
join in its destruction. He resisted the secession conspiracy; but his southern pro-slavery prejudices also imbued
him with the prevalent antagonism to the Republican party.
He therefore nursed a scheme to carry Texas back into independent sovereignty, and, with her territory and population
as a basis, to undertake the conquest and annexation of
Mexico.

But the conspirators, ignoring all restraint, without a
shadow of legality, assembled a revolutionary State convention, and on February 1st passed an ordinance of secession,
with a provision submitting it to a popular vote. Houston,
pursuing his side intrigue, approved a joint resolution of
the State Legislature (February 4th) to legalize the convention, but accompanied his approval with a protest that it
should have no effect except to elicit public decision on the
single question of adherence to the Union. When in due

time an alleged vote (taken on February 23d) ratifying the ordinance was submitted to him, he refused to recognize further acts of the convention; whereupon the enraged convention (March 16th) declared his office vacant, and empowered the lieutenant-governor to seize the executive authority.

Meanwhile General Twiggs, commanding the Federal troops in Texas, by treasonable connivance, on February 18th surrendered the military posts and property to a hasty collection of about a regiment of rebels in arms, purporting to act by authority of the convention, and set the various scattered detachments of the army in motion to evacuate the State. Before this had taken place, the newly inaugurated Lincoln administration sent a messenger to Houston, who was still reputed by public rumor to be loyal, and offered to concentrate a strong body of the United States troops under the new commander, Colonel Waite, form an entrenched camp, and sustain his authority as governor. Houston, however (March 29th), refused the offer; and having neither the United States Government nor the people of Texas to lean upon, the conspirators relentlessly pushed him into an ignoble obscurity and transferred the State to the military domination of the Rebellion.

Thus, by easy stages and successive usurpations of authority, rebellion accomplished the first step of its operations unmolested and unopposed. South Carolina, as we have seen, seceded on December 20, 1860; Mississippi on January 9, 1861; Florida on January 10th; Alabama on January 11th; Georgia on January 19th; Louisiana on January 26th; and Texas on February 1st. The various ordinances are in substance that devised and adopted by South Carolina. All the States put on the airs of independent republics, though this pretence was of short duration, as was designed and arranged by the conspiracy.

But the mere perversion of elections, the adoption of a secession ordinance, and the assumption of independent authority, was not enough for the Cotton Republics. Though they hoped to evade civil war by shrewd intrigue, they well understood they had no certain immunity from it. It was therefore essential to possess the arms and military posts within their borders. There were in the seceded States one quite extensive navy-yard, at Pensacola, Florida; twelve to fifteen harbor-forts along the Atlantic and Gulf coasts, capable of mounting a thousand guns, and having cost over five millions; half a dozen arsenals, containing an aggregate of one hundred and fifteen thousand arms, transferred there from northern arsenals by Secretary Floyd about a year before, on pretence of danger from slave insurrections. In addition there were three mints, four important custom-houses, three revenue-cutters on duty at the several seaports, and a variety of other miscellaneous property. This estimate does not include the already mentioned public property surrendered by General Twiggs in Texas, which of itself formed an aggregate of eighteen military posts and stations, and arms and stores to a large amount and value.

This property had been purchased with the money of the Federal Government; the land on which the buildings stood, though perhaps in some instances donated, was vested in the United States, not only by the right of eminent domain, but also by formal legislative deeds of cession from the States themselves.

It was now assumed that the heresy of State supremacy, through which the States pretended to derive their authority to pass secession ordinances, also restored to them the right of eminent domain, or that they had always retained it; that therefore they might, under the law of nations, justifiably take possession, holding themselves responsible in money damages to be settled by negotiation. The hypothesis and its parent dogma were of course both palpably false and absurd. The Government of the United States, unlike other great nations, has steadily opposed the maintenance of a large military force in time of peace. The whole regular army amounted to only a little over seventeen thousand men. These, as usual, were mainly occupied in defence of the western frontier against hostile Indian tribes. Consequently, but three of these southern forts were garrisoned, and they by only about a company each. An equal force was stationed for the protection of the arsenals at Augusta, Ga., Mt. Vernon, Ala., and Baton Rouge, La.

As a necessary part of the conspiracy, the governors of the Cotton States now, by official order to their extemporized militia companies, took forcible possession of these forts, arsenals, navy-yard, custom-houses, and other property, in many cases even before their secession ordinances were passed. This was nothing less than levying actual war against the United States, though as yet attended by no violence or bloodshed. The ordinary process was, the sudden appearance of a superior armed force, a demand for surrender in the name of the State, and the compliance under protest by the officer in charge—salutes to the flag, peaceable evacuation, and unmolested transit home being graciously permitted as military courtesy. To this course of procedure three exceptions occurred: first, no attempt was made against Fort Taylor at Key West, Fort Jefferson on Tortugas Island, and Fort Pickens at Pensacola, on account of the distance and danger; second, part of the troops in Texas were eventually refused the promised transit and captured; and third, the forts in Charleston Harbor underwent peculiar vicissitudes, to be specially narrated in the next chapter.

CHAPTER II.

CHARLESTON HARBOR.

CONSPIRACY was not confined to South Carolina or the Cotton States; unfortunately, it had established itself in the highest official circles of the national administration. Three members of President Buchanan's cabinet—Cobb of Georgia, Secretary of the Treasury, Floyd of Virginia, Secretary of War, and Thompson of Mississippi, Secretary of the Interior— had become ardent and active disunionists. Grouped about these three principal traitors were a number of subordinate and yet influential functionaries, all forming together a central secession cabal, working, in daily and flagrant violation of their official oaths, to promote the success of the Southern conspiracy. After the meeting of Congress, on the first Monday of December, the Senators and Representatives from the Cotton States were in Washington to counsel, prompt, and assist this cabinet cabal, and the President was subjected to the double influence of insidious suggestion from within, and personal pressure from without his administration, acting in regulated concert.

No taint of disloyal purpose or thought appears to attach to President Buchanan; but his condition of mind predisposed him in a remarkable degree to fall under the controlling influence of his disloyal counsellors. He possessed the opposing qualities of feeble will and stubborn prejudice; advancing years and decreasing vigor added to his irresolu·

tion and embarrassed his always limited capabilities. In the defeat of Breckenridge, whom he had championed, and in the sweeping success of the Republicans, he had suffered scorching rebuke and deep humiliation. His administration was condemned, his policy was overthrown; his proud party was a hopeless wreck. He had no elasticity of mind, no buoyancy of hope to recover from the shock. Withal he had a blind disbelief in the popular judgment; he refused to recognize the fact of an adverse decision at the ballot-box. After his long affiliation with Southern men in thought and action, he saw, as it were, through Southern eyes; his mind dwelt painfully on the fancied wrongs of the South. His natural impulse, therefore, was to embarrass and thwart the Republican victory by such official utterance and administration as would occur in his brief remainder of office; and this was probably also the first and natural feeling of even the loyal members of his Cabinet, who were prominent and devoted Democratic partisans.

The presidential election decided, it was necessary to begin the preparation of his annual message to Congress, which would convene in less than a month. Just about this time came the thickening reports of Southern insurrection and the ostentatious resignations of the Charleston Federal officials. The first expressions from loyal members of the Cabinet were that rebellion must be put down. But this remedy grated harshly on Buchanan's partisan prejudices. He had aided these Southern malcontents to intrigue for slavery, to complain of oppression, to threaten disunion. To become the public accuser of his late allies and friends, under disaster and defeat, doubtless seemed desertion and black ingratitude. The Cabinet traitors had no such scruples. They were ready enough to desert the President, but they wanted first to use him.

When, on December 3d, the President's message was laid before Congress, it was found to contain the most unjust and indefensible allegations, the most glaringly inconsistent and irreconcilable doctrines, the most childish and useless suggestions. He charged that Southern discontent was caused by "long-continued and intemperate interference of the Northern people with the question of slavery in the Southern States," in face of the well-known fact that Southern interference in free territory was the cause of the crisis. He declared that, while a State had no right to secede, the Constitution gave no right to coerce a State into submission when it had withdrawn, or was attempting to withdraw, from the confederacy. This was raising a false issue. The question was not of acting against a State for either constitutional or unconstitutional efforts, but of suppressing insurrection and punishing individuals for violation of United States laws. Finally, he argued that, to enforce United States laws, a United States Court must first issue a writ and a United States Marshal execute it; and that where judges and marshals had resigned, and a universal popular feeling opposed, such execution became impossible. In this he ignored the fact that he had power to instantly appoint new judges and marshals, and make the whole army, navy, and militia of the nation a *posse comitatus* to execute their process; and within one month after signing this message, he, himself, actually nominated a citizen of Pennsylvania Collector of the Port of Charleston, in signal defiance of his own theory. As a fitting climax to such puerile reasoning, he urged an amendment of the Constitution that would give slavery the very concession in repudiation of which the people had just overwhelmingly elected Lincoln. As a specimen of absurdity, stupidity, and wilful wrong-headedness, this message is not equalled in American political literature. For this extraordinary state paper, which effectually tied the hands of the administration and opened to rebellion a pathway free from obstruction or danger, the trio of conspirators in the Cabinet, Cobb, Floyd, and Thompson, may be reasonably held responsible. How they beguiled a President of waning mental powers and naturally feeble purpose, may be easily enough imagined; but how they silenced the honest logic of their loyal colleagues, is yet one of the riddles of history.

The first and chief solicitude of the South Carolinians was to gain possession of the Charleston forts. To secede, to organize their little State into a miniature republic, was indeed a vast achievement in their own eyes; but they were shrewd enough to perceive that their claim to independence and sovereignty would be ridiculed by the family of nations if they could not control their own and only seaport. That alone would give them a free highway to the world at large; with that they could offer the benefits of commerce, security from tempests, refuge from the perils of war, to ships of other nations; could negotiate advantageous treaties, and perhaps conclude powerful alliances. "We must have the forts" was therefore the watchword of the secret caucus; and before long, from every street-corner in Charleston, came the impatient echo, "The forts must be ours."

The city of Charleston lies on a tongue of land between the Ashley and Cooper rivers; from their confluence the bay extends eastward some four miles to the open sea. Three forts defend the harbor. The first and smallest is Castle Pinckney, an old-time structure of brick, and of insignificant strength in modern warfare. It lies one mile from the city; it was capable of holding a war garrison of 100 men; and its armament of twenty-two guns was at the time complete. Farther out is the second in size and importance,

Fort Moultrie, situated on Sullivan's Island, some four miles from the city, very near the mouth of the harbor, on its northern side. It dates back in name and heroic reputation to the Revolution, when, however, it was little else than an extemporized battery of palmetto-logs and sand. In modern times it has been rebuilt in brick, under scientific construction, and though lying disadvantageously low, it had been changed into an effective channel defence, capable of mounting fifty-five guns en barbette and holding a garrison of 300 men. The third and most important work was

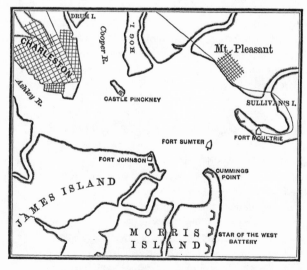

Map of Charleston Harbor.

Fort Sumter, also of brick, but of more imposing size. It was situated about the middle of the harbor entrance, and back half a mile from its mouth; it was erected on a shoal

raised to an artificial island; the walls were eight feet thick
and forty feet high, with two tiers of casemates; it was five-
sided, enclosing a space of about 300 by 350 feet, and in its
casemates and on its rampart it was designed for 140 guns;
its proper war-garrison was 650 men. In addition to these
forts in the harbor, there were two government buildings
in the city of Charleston: the Custom-House and the United States Arsenal, the latter containing a total of 22,430
arms.

To guard and hold possession of this property, there were
in the arsenal a military storekeeper and fourteen enlisted
men. Castle Pinckney was occupied only by an ordnance
sergeant and his family; Fort Sumter by one or two engineer officers, employing one hundred and ten workmen in re-
pairs; Fort Moultrie alone, in addition to another party of
fifty workmen employed by the engineer officer in charge,
had a garrison of sixty-nine soldiers and nine officers under
Major Robert Anderson, who had command of the whole
harbor and all the forts. The walls of Moultrie were low,
and at one place almost submerged in the drifting sand-
banks of Sullivan's Island; a storming party, the commandant reported, could run like rats over the ramparts. Parties of Charlestonians frequently visited it to spy out its
weak points; volunteer companies were organized in the
city for the expedition of capture; scaling-ladders were prepared to make the attempt a certainty; the talk of the street-
rabble and the newspapers made no concealment of their
exulting confidence that they held Moultrie in the hollow
of their hand. Hospitable fire-eaters went even so far as to
invite Major Anderson to comfortable dinners, and to tell
him, in confidential frankness over their wine, that they re-
spected him as an officer and loved him as a Southerner, but
that they "must have the fort."

For the time being, however, the inner councils of the conspiracy seem to have frowned upon any rash or premature attempt upon Moultrie, and to have sagely relied on obtaining possession through intrigue and negotiation, since the latter method would not carry with it any danger of reprisal or punishment. A most important advantage in this direction had already been gained by Mr. Buchanan's adoption of the doctrine of non-coercion ; the next essential step was to prevent any reinforcements from coming into Charleston Harbor.

Though not perhaps susceptible of historical proof, strong inference warrants the belief that Floyd, Secretary of War, inspired by the Washington cabal of traitors, procured the appointment of Anderson to the command with the hope that as a Southern man he would lend himself to an easy surrender of the forts. To Floyd, also, seems to have been committed the further supervision of the intrigues respecting them. He still avowed himself a unionist ; but he disproved his public declarations by a steady series of services and favors to the rebellion, of whose design he could not have remained in ignorance.

Congress had met, the message had been delivered, the fatal doctrine of non-coercion conceded by the President and adopted as an administration policy. Under its protecting promises treason not only proceeded with accelerated organization in the Cotton States, but made its avowals, its boasts, and its threats in Congress. South Carolina and secession were the topics of the hour—Moultrie and Anderson the central and growing objects of anxiety ; and at length the North, through its senators and representatives, and still more loudly through its newspaper press, began to bring its influence upon the President for reinforcement and preparation. At the same time the secessionists congregated at Washington were no less alert and active ; they obtained

Buchanan's tacit promise that he would send no reinforcements unless Moultrie were attacked, and had hampered Anderson with confidential instructions from Floyd, to take no offensive measures until in the nature of things, through a sudden assault, he would be overwhelmed and powerless.

These conflicting efforts brought on a Cabinet crisis and forced the President to a direct official decision. General Cass, the Secretary of State, had his home in Michigan; and feeling the stiffening influence of Northwestern sentiment, and having, besides, his own somewhat sluggish though patriotic blood roused by the high-handed and unchecked intrigues of the conspirators, began to insist that reinforcements be sent to Charleston. Buchanan becoming also a trifle anxious over the situation, sent for Floyd. Floyd, suave and deceitful, dallied, evaded, pooh-poohed the danger, had resort to chivalric bombast. The South Carolinians, he said, were honorable gentlemen. They would scorn to take the forts. They must not be irritated. At length, finding the President growing unusually obstinate in his new fancy, Floyd sought refuge in the suggestion that General Scott be consulted. Scott was a Virginian; Floyd secretly thought he would fall in with the current secession drift, and perhaps officially advise the surrender or evacuation of the forts to "conciliate" South Carolina.

General Scott, scarcely able to rise from his sick bed in New York, hastened to Washington on December 12th. Floyd had hitherto with studied neglect kept him excluded from knowledge of War Department affairs; but now, for the first time consulted, and recognizing the gravity of the situation, the General heartily joined Cass in recommending that reinforcements be instantly sent.

Floyd was surprised, disappointed, disconcerted. He summarily rejected the advice of Scott, as he had opposed that of Cass. Seizing adroitly upon a phrase of Buchanan's message, which affirmed the duty of the President to protect public property, he said: True, it is simply a question of property. You need no army to assert that. Place an ordnance sergeant in the fort; he will represent the sovereignty and the proprietary rights of the United States as well as a regiment. This was a subtle and skilful thrust. Mr. Buchanan's slow intellect was both flattered and confused by having his own misstatement of a vital political principle quoted and turned upon him. He had not the wit to rejoin that neither political sovereignty nor proprietary right were longer complete if possession was once lost. Nevertheless, Buchanan had a dim consciousness of treachery. He continued to plead with his secretary that he ought to send reinforcements; warning him that a loss of the forts under the circumstances would cover the name of Floyd "with an infamy that all time can never efface."

Floyd was well nigh in despair. He turned upon the President all his florid Southern rhetoric, all the final armory of offended Southern dignity, and the ever-ready threats of Southern resort to violence. Send troops to Charleston, he concluded, and the swarming and enraged South Carolinians would not leave one brick of Moultrie upon another. Nor was Floyd content to risk the issue upon his own eloquence. He gave the note of alarm to every prominent traitor in Washington, and without delay they flocked around the doubting, hesitating President—Hunter, Mason, Jefferson Davis—the whole busy cabal of plotting, caucusing conspirators, filling him alternately with such deceitful promises of good behavior and such terrible visions of revolutionary violence, that Mr. Buchanan was both frightened and soothed into a reluctant compliance with their advice. It was the scene of the wily Vivien and the yielding Merlin re-enacted;

I.—2

and while the Sage of Wheatland slept in doting confidence,
every conspiring secessionist cried "Fool!" and wrought

> "the charm
> Of woven paces and of waving hands,"

to complete their secret web of conspiracy.

The issue was decided in the Cabinet meeting of December
13th; after a spirited re-argument, the President told his
Secretary of State that he was sorry to differ with him, but
that he could not order reinforcements to Charleston; whereupon General Cass tendered his resignation and retired from
official life. Cobb had resigned from the Cabinet a few days
before. Black, the Attorney-General, was now made Secretary of State; Thomas of Maryland, Secretary of the Treasury; and Edwin M. Stanton appointed Attorney-General.

If Mr. Buchanan flattered himself that his concession to
Floyd, Davis, and the cabal, would stay the tide of disunion
in the South, he was quickly undeceived. At the very time
the Cabinet meeting was holding its final discussion of the
question of reinforcements, a mysterious paper was being
circulated for signature through the two houses of Congress,
and on the second day following, the newspapers which announced the retirement of Cass also contained the first definite and authentic proclamation of concerted revolution by
the Cotton States, and the proposal to form a Southern republic.* It was a brief document, but pregnant with all the

---

* "TO OUR CONSTITUENTS.

"WASHINGTON, December 14, 1860.

"The argument is exhausted. All hope of relief in the Union, through the
agency of committees, congressional legislation, or constitutional amendments, is
extinguished, and we trust the South will not be deceived by appearances or the
pretence of new guarantees. In our judgment the Republicans are resolute in
the purpose to grant nothing that will or ought to satisfy the South. We are
satisfied the honor, safety, and independence of the Southern people require the

essential purposes of the conspiracy. It was signed by about
one-half the Senators and Representatives from the States of
North Carolina, South Carolina, Georgia, Alabama, Mississippi, Louisiana, Florida, Texas, and Arkansas, and is the
" official " beginning of the subsequent " Confederate States,"
just as Gist's October circular was the " official " beginning
of South Carolina secession.

On the fifth day after the publication of this manifesto, the
South Carolina Convention passed, signed, and published its
ordinance of secession, as already related ; and now it was
resolved to demand possession of the Charleston forts as an
incident of sovereignty and independence. It was assumed
that the President would not refuse to yield them up after
peaceful diplomatic negotiation, and upon an offer to account for them as property in a regular business settlement
between the two governments. The convention, acting upon this theory, appointed three commissioners to proceed
to Washington to treat for the delivery of the forts, maga-
zines, light-houses, and other real estate, for an apportion-
ment of the public debt, for a division of all other property,
and generally to negotiate about other measures and arrangements.

All this proceeded with the decorum and mock solemnity

---

organization of a Southern confederacy—a result to be obtained only by separate
State secession—that the primary object of each slaveholding State ought to be its
speedy and absolute separation from a Union with hostile States."

(Signed by :

Representatives Pugh, Clopton, Moore, Curry, and Stallworth, of Alabama ;
Senator Iverson and Representatives Underwood, Gartrell, Jackson, Jones,
and Crawford, of Georgia ; Representative Hawkins, of Florida ; Representative Hindman, of Arkansas ; Senators Jefferson Davis and A. G. Brown,
and Representatives Barksdale, Singleton, and Reuben Davis, of Mississippi ;
Representatives Craige and Ruffin, of North Carolina ; Senators Slidell and
Benjamin, and Representative Landrum, of Louisiana ; Senators Wigfall
and Hemphill, and Representative Reagan, of Texas ; Representatives Bonham, Miles, McQueen, and Ashmore, of South Carolina.)

in which children play at kings and queens. The commissioners reached Washington on December 26th, and Mr. Buchanan, with all the curiosity and palpitation of an actor in a new drama, seems to have looked upon it not as the miserable farce of conspiracy which it was, but as a real piece of government business. The commissioners immediately made their presence known, and the President appointed an interview for them at one o'clock next day. Before that hour arrived, however, news of a totally unlooked-for event gave their intended negotiation an entirely new direction and result.

That event was the sudden military movement by Major Anderson, transferring his entire garrison from Fort Moultrie to Fort Sumter, in Charleston Harbor, on the night of the commissioners' arrival in Washington, December 26. Daily observation left him no doubt that Moultrie was to be assaulted; every day strengthened the design, increased the preparation, augmented the drilled and undrilled forces to be joined in the undertaking. There was no longer hope that the President would heed his repeated calls and send him reinforcements. There was, however, one resource yet available. Sumter was the real key to the harbor. Captain Foster and his engineer force of workmen and mechanics had now prepared it for occupancy, and could soon make it ready for defence. Its guns commanded Moultrie. There was no approach to it except by boats, and, for a time, at least, he would be beyond the reach of the Charleston mob and its improvised scaling-ladders. Thoughts like these, long-present and familiar to his mind, were once more carefully revolved and re-examined, when on Christmas night he returned from a neighboring holiday merrymaking to his somewhat cheerless quarters in Moultrie; and before he retired to his sleep, he took his secret resolve to abandon Moultrie and take post in Sumter.

The 26th of December was a busy day for the commandant. There were vessels to be hired, and an excuse invented to send away the families, the baggage, the unnumbered *impedimenta* of the garrison. For this, one or two chosen staff-officers must be let into the secret. Finally, boats must be provided and concealed on the beach, in which to cross the men. Anderson's personal care was extended to every detail, and every item of preparation moved like clock-work. The families and baggage were got off in the afternoon. A sunset parade of the men was ordered, ostensibly to be on the alert against assault, a species of exercise with which the garrison had become somewhat sorely familiar. The supper stood smoking on the officers' mess-table, when Captain Doubleday, second in command, was hastily called to Major Anderson, who now for the first time told him that he must have his company under arms and ready to march to the beach in twenty minutes. Everything proceeded as had been arranged, without delay and without accident; even the rebel guard-boats, which had recently been set to patrolling the bay to render such a movement impossible, failed to make any discovery. By nine o'clock that night the transfer was an assured success; the officers sat down to eat the supper in Sumter which had been cooked for them in Moultrie. A small detail of men and an officer were left behind to spike guns, burn carriages, cut down the flag-staff, and to complete during the night the removal of needed supplies; they finished their work and joined their comrades in Sumter a little after sunrise next morning.

This movement filled the Union sentiment of the country with the liveliest exultation. It was a spontaneous, uncalculating act of patriotism which will enshrine the name of Anderson in grateful recollection so long as American history shall be read. Advance news of the event was sent from

Charleston to the commissioners on the morning of December 27th; and they immediately communicated it to Mr. Buchanan, whom it threw into a most embarrassing perplexity. He postponed the commissioners' interview, and summoned his Cabinet to consider the situation. Floyd at once declared the movement to be in violation of orders; and the President himself, in his chagrin that his Southern friends should have a new burden of complaint, was half-inclined to peremptorily order Anderson back to Moultrie. He was prudent enough, however, to suspend his judgment until Anderson could be heard; for he had lately become cognizant of the equivocal and double-tongued instructions which Floyd, without his knowledge, had sent him, and which he inferred might at least technically justify Anderson's movement.

On Friday, December 28th, he gave the commissioners their promised interview. Mr. Buchanan, himself, writes that "on their introduction he stated that he could recognize them only as private gentlemen, and not as commissioners from a sovereign State; that it was to Congress, and to Congress alone, they must appeal. He nevertheless expressed his willingness to communicate to that body, as the only competent tribunal, any propositions they might have to offer." He does not appear to have realized that this proposal was in reality a quasi-recognition of South Carolina's claim to independence, and a misdemeanor meriting impeachment.

What is a thousand times more astounding, however, is that, on their part, the commissioners were too stupid to perceive the vast advantage of this concession and offer. It would have placed the President before the public, and before foreign powers especially, in the attitude of their apologist, if not their advocate. It would have committed him to refrain from any hostile action against South Carolina during the pendency of such debate as the proposition might provoke in Congress. It would have thrust a firebrand into Congress, to complicate and divide every faction and element in politics except their own friends ; in short, it would have made Washington City the principal centre of revolution. Fortunately for the country, their blindness lost to secession its only possible chance of peaceful success.

Under the impression that Mr. Buchanan was completely within the domination of the Cabinet cabal, the commissioners made an angry complaint against Anderson, and haughtily demanded "explanations," threatening that, if these were not satisfactory, they would suspend their negotiations. Such a threat from applicants for recognition and favor was the very acme of stupidity and maladdress.

Anderson little suspected—perhaps never knew—how narrowly he escaped disavowal and disgrace by the President of the United States, for his act of fidelity and patriotism. The conspirators had shrewdly calculated on their influence over Mr. Buchanan. For two days he hesitated, leaning evidently to the counsels of his secession advisers. There were protracted Cabinet sessions, acrimonious debates, and a final struggle between the President's disloyal counsellors from the South and the loyal ones from the North, over the possession and control of their temporizing, vacillating chief. It was not till the latter were on the point of resigning that the President was brought to a direct decision against the conspirators ; even then, but for an outside complication, the result might have been doubtful. For about a week Floyd and Thompson had both been in bad odor. A transaction, in which near a million dollars' worth of Indian Trust Bonds were abstracted from a safe in the Interior Department and replaced by Floyd's premature acceptances, looked so much like official theft that it was occupying the attention of the courts and greatly exercising the mind of the President.

The spell was finally broken on December 31st, when Mr. Buchanan accepted Floyd's resignation, which the latter reluctantly tendered on the 29th; he also sent the commissioners their definite answer, namely: that, whatever might have been his first inclination, the Governor of South Carolina had, since Anderson's movement, forcibly seized Fort Moultrie, Castle Pinckney, and the Charleston Arsenal, Custom-House, and Post-Office, and covered them with the Palmetto flag; that under such circumstances he could not and would not withdraw the Federal troops from Sumter. This ended the rebel mission. They departed abruptly for home, leaving behind them an insolent rejoinder to the President's letter, charging him with tacit consent to the scheme of peaceable secession.

Governor Pickens (newly chosen by the Legislature, December 14th) was perhaps the most daring revolutionist in South Carolina, and as commander-in-chief of the State forces he at once assumed and exercised dictatorial powers. Within three or four days after his seizure of the forts he ordered the selection of suitable points on the islands forming the bay, and the commencement of batteries to command the ship-channels against reinforcements. It was the beginning of the long and eventful siege of Sumter. Moultrie was soon restored to its offensive powers; Castle Pinckney passed into his hands undamaged; with a working force of volunteers impelled by fanatical zeal, supplemented by the more efficient labor of large gangs of slaves freely furnished from the city and plantations of the neighborhood, battery after battery rose around Anderson's stronghold, unmolested and unchecked for three long months, until, in an encompassing ring of fire, and under the sheer overweight of metal and numbers, the proud flag of Sumter went down in temporary humiliation. And that the drama should not lack its interludes of grotesque farce, all through this continuation of contumacy, insurrection, rampart-building, gun-planting, and actual repeated firing on the flag of the United States, the "Republic" of South Carolina, through its governor, its legislature, its convention, and its partisans, clamorously insisted and reiterated that the Government was waging war upon it.

The Cabinet crisis of December 31st, and the retirement of Floyd, greatly changed the attitude of the Government toward rebellion. Holt was made Secretary of War, and became at once the Hercules of the national defence. Black, though as Attorney-General he had in November written an official opinion against coercion, was so far changed that he now zealously advocated the reinforcement of Sumter. All the unionists of the Cabinet—Black, Holt, Stanton, even Toucey in a mild way, and not long afterward Dix with memorable vigor—joined heartily in preparation to vindicate the national authority. General Scott was placed in military control; and the President, being for a period kept by loyal advice in a more patriotic mood, permitted various precautionary measures to be taken, among which, a well-designed, though finally abortive effort to reinforce Sumter, was perhaps the most noteworthy.

Various plans to send men and provisions to Anderson were discussed, and it was at last decided to attempt stratagem. A swift merchant-steamer, the "Star of the West" was chartered in New York, loaded with the needed supplies and two hundred and fifty recruits; thus prepared, she sailed on her errand on the night of January 5, 1861. The effort to keep the expedition an entire secret had not succeeded. Notice of her departure went to Charleston from New York; and in addition to this, Thompson, the conspiring Secretary of the Interior, who at the last moment learned the fact in Cabinet

meeting, also warned his Charleston friends of her coming.
Anderson does not seem to have received his notice, though
he gathered from newspapers that some such enterprise
was being matured. He was, therefore, not greatly surprised, when on the morning of January 9th he was hastily
informed that a strange vessel was entering the harbor,
and hurrying upon the rampart, saw her steaming up the
channel in the direction of Sumter. She presented no warlike appearance; men and supplies were hidden below decks.
But in these nine days of January the rebels had repaired
Moultrie and completed one or two sand-batteries at the
harbor entrance, and, thoroughly informed of the character
and destination of the vessel, they began a vigorous fire
upon her as soon as she came within range. At this, finding
concealment no longer important, her captain ran up a large
United States flag, a signal which dispelled all doubts Anderson may have had that she indeed came to bring him the
wished-for relief. He gave orders to man his guns and prepare to fire on the batteries ; meanwhile the steamer, though
hit once or twice, had passed the first batteries without
serious damage. Now, however, the course of the channel
would oblige her to steam directly toward the ready guns
of Moultrie, and the sight of this new peril seems to have
daunted the courage of the officer in charge. Anderson saw
with deep chagrin that, just as he was ready to cheer and
greet the new-comer by returning the rebel fire, the steamer
suddenly slackened her speed, then put about, and ran once
more unharmed past the rebel batteries and through the hostile cannon-balls out to sea.

Anderson's blood was hot with the insult his own eyes had
witnessed to the flag and sovereignty of the United States.
He sat down and wrote a brief note to the Governor of South
Carolina, demanding to know if the firing on the vessel and

the flag had been by his order, and declaring that, unless the act were disclaimed, he would close the harbor with the guns of Sumter. It would have been better to have left the threat unuttered. Governor Pickens was more than a match for him in bravado; he immediately avowed and justified the act. Anderson in a second note so far receded as to say that he had made up his mind to first ask his government for instructions, and requested safe-conduct for a bearer of dispatches. This emboldened the governor to a second trial of bluster; next day he sent Anderson a formal demand for the surrender of Sumter. Anderson replied rather meekly that he could not comply with the demand; but that, if the governor saw fit "to refer this matter to Washington," he would depute an officer to accompany the messenger.

The Charleston conspirators, never at a loss to talk or intrigue, were really not yet ready to fight. They caught eagerly at this truce which Anderson offered them; it would renew the negotiations which their commissioners had so unceremoniously abandoned; above all, it would afford them ample time to complete their harbor batteries and collect troops against further expeditions of reinforcement or attack. On January 12th, therefore, I. W. Hayne, the Attorney-General of South Carolina, proceeded to Washington as an envoy to carry to President Buchanan the governor's demand for the surrender of Sumter, with authority to give in return the pledge "that the valuation of such property will be accounted for by this State upon the adjustment of its relations with the United States."

Hayne had, however, scarcely reached his destination when a superior influence took control of him and his mission. By the middle of January most of the Cotton States had passed ordinances of secession, seized the undefended military posts within their limits, and were addressing each other as independent States. But no amount of official vaporing or local ostentation could convince even themselves of either dignity or power; especially it could not, in the eyes of the world, magnify petty cotton republics into serious importance or influence. However they might temporarily paralyze the laws of the Union, the constitutional rights of the nation were unbroken, and the military power of the Government slumbered like a mighty giant. To brave his terrible awakening the necessity of early combination in some system of common defence was too apparent to need argument. The senators and representatives of seceded States, though some of them had already withdrawn from Congress, were yet lingering in Washington as the most central point for observation and consultation. The formation of a Southern confederacy was, from the first, a recognized purpose, announced in their manifesto of December 14th, and again repeated in letters from a secret caucus held January 5th.

Indeed, the whole programme probably dated back to the early days of the session, when it may be presumed the plan was elaborated by a few of the leading spirits. So far, though some of their combinations had failed, yet in the main the scheme had moved on with ever-growing strength from success to success. By the middle of January the conspirators in Washington realized that they must hurry the completion of their organization during the brief continuance of the expiring administration. Even the belligerent Governor Pickens was made to understand the advantage of such a course. "Mr. Lincoln," he wrote, "cannot possibly do more for us than Mr. Buchanan has done." When therefore, most unexpectedly, South Carolina obtained through Anderson's offer a new chance to propose negotiation, the central cabal at Washington resolved to make it the means of gaining time to set a common provisional government in motion, without on their part furnishing the pretext for any military movement which might threaten or check their plans. They therefore met in a caucus, and appointed a committee consisting of Senators Fitzpatrick, Mallory, and Slidell; this committee began and carried on a dilatory correspondence with Mr. Hayne and with the President, which they managed to prolong into February, all that while keeping open the Anderson truce by the assumption that negotiations were pending. Mr. Buchanan, always indisposed to act, always welcoming any excuse to postpone decision, fell easily into the toils of this side intrigue for delay. Some of his counsellors must have seen through the transparent game with much impatience, for the whole affair was at last rather abruptly ended. On February 6th, Secretary Holt wrote for the President to Hayne, that neither the proposed sale of Fort Sumter, nor its relinquishment under South Carolina's claim of eminent domain, could for a moment be thought of, since it was not a mere question of property, as had been assumed, but involved political rights of the highest national importance. This closed the correspondence, and Hayne went home to report the second failure to obtain the forts by diplomacy.

But the conspirators had gained their main point. This negotiation paralyzed and postponed all the plans and preparations to send help to Anderson, upon which some of the Cabinet members had labored with zeal and earnestness; while on the other hand, on February 4th, two days preceding Hayne's dismissal, the Provisional Congress of the rebel States assembled at Montgomery, Ala., and by the 18th of that month had completed and inaugurated the provisional government under which the local insurrections of the Cotton States became an organized rebellion against the government of the Union.

Nor was this the only advantage which the conspiracy had secured. Since the 12th of January a condition of things existed in the harbor of Pensacola, Fla., similar to that at Charleston. The insurgents had threatened, and the officer in charge had surrendered the Pensacola Navy Yard. Lieutenant Slemmer, of the army, with a little garrison of forty-six men, held Fort Barrancas. Finding he could not defend his post, nor Fort McRee, also on the mainland, he, with a loyal courage which will ever render his name illustrious, repeated the strategy of Anderson, and moved his slender command, augmented by thirty ordinary seamen from the navy yard, on the morning of January 10th, to Fort Pickens, a large and more defensible work standing at the harbor entrance, on the western end of Santa Rosa Island. The Government hurriedly sent a few ships of war to assist him, while the rebels began gathering an army to assault the fort. Under cover of the Hayne negotiation, Senator Mallory managed to draw the President into an agreement, embodied in formal orders dated January 29th, that Fort Pickens should not be reinforced unless it were assaulted by the rebels, or preparations were made to do so.

The Hayne business disposed of, there was once more a little flurry of war consultations at the Executive Mansion to devise and dispatch a new expedition to reinforce Sumter. This time a few small vessels belonging to the Coast Survey were to be assembled and placed under command of Captain Ward, of the navy, for that purpose; the details of the plan do not appear to have transpired. But the President's energetic moods were lamentably short; by the 23d of February this scheme, also, was definitely abandoned, probably for the overruling reason that but nine days remained of Mr. Buchanan's presidential term.

CHAPTER III.

THE CONFEDERATE STATES' REBELLION.

On the fourth day of February, 1861, while the Peace Conference met in Washington to consider propositions of compromise and concession, the delegates of the seceding States convened in Montgomery, Ala., to combine and solidify the general conspiracy into an organized and avowed rebellion.

Such action had been arranged and agreed upon from the beginning. The congressional manifesto from Washington, as far back as December 14th, advised that " we are satisfied the honor, safety, and independence of the Southern people require the organization of a Southern confederacy—a result to be obtained only by separate State secession." This agreement of the Washington caucus was steadily adhered to. The specious argument invented in Georgia, that " we can make better terms outside of the Union than in it," and the public declaration of Mississippi's commissioner in Baltimore, that secession " was not taken with the view of breaking up the present government, but to assure to her (Mississippi) those guarantees and principles of liberty which had been pledged to her by the fathers of the Revolution," were but tricks of the conspiracy for local use and effect. The managers well understood that if the States were once committed to secession, the mere revolutionary momentum of the crisis would carry them to whatever combination they might devise.

The whole plan appears to have been more fully matured and adopted in a Washington caucus held on the night of January 5, 1861, at which time four important points were arranged : 1st, the Cotton States should immediately secede ; 2d, that delegates should be chosen to meet in Montgomery, "to organize a confederacy," not later than February 15th ; 3d, that the conspirators would remain in Congress as long as possible, to obstruct coercive legislation; and 4th, that Jefferson Davis, Slidell, and Mallory be appointed a committee to carry out the objects of the caucus.   Thus, more than a month before his inauguration as rebel president, the leader of the conspiracy was entrusted with the supervision and management of the plot.   The caucus programme was executed with but slight deviation.   The States seceded, appointed delegates to Montgomery, and the conspirators withdrew from Congress at the last moment to assume the more active control of the rebellion in their respective States.

As events progressed it became evident to the leaders that it was important to complete their new government before the expiration of Mr. Buchanan's term.   They understood perfectly his temper and purpose.   Though he denied them the treasonable complicity they had hoped and asked, and discontinued the important concessions with which he began, he still stood committed to non-coercion.   What his successor might decide was uncertain.   Repeated efforts had been made to draw from Lincoln some expression of his intention —some forecast of his policy, but they had been uniformly unsuccessful.

Accordingly the secession delegates met in Montgomery on February 4th, instead of the 15th, as had been first arranged, and organized a provisional Congress, and a few days thereafter (February 8, 1861) adopted a provisional government, to be known as "The Confederate States of America." There was little difficulty in arriving at this result; most if not all the seceders' State conventions had declared a wish that their proposed new government should be modelled on that of the United States.

From this they proceeded to the work of framing a permanent constitution. This was a somewhat slower process, though it was also completed and adopted by the provisional Congress on March 11, 1861. Few changes from the Constitution of the United States were made. The new constitution professed to be established by "each State acting in its sovereign and independent character," instead of simply by "We the people." It provided that in newly acquired territory "the institution of negro slavery, as it now exists in the Confederate States, shall be recognized and protected by Congress and by the Territorial Government"; also for the right of transit and sojourn for "slaves and other property," and the right to reclaim "slaves and other persons" to service or labor. It did not, as consistency required, provide for the right of secession or deny the right of coercion; on the contrary all its implications were against the former and in favor of the latter, for it declared itself to be the supreme law of the land, binding on the judges in every State. It provided for the punishment of treason; and declared that no State should enter into any treaty, alliance, or confederation, grant letters of marque and reprisal, coin money, lay duties, keep troops or ships of war in time of peace, make any compact with another State or with a foreign power—a sweeping practical negation of the whole heretical dogma of State supremacy upon which they had built their revolt.

The day after the rebel Congress adopted its provisional government, it elected (February 9, 1861) Jefferson Davis, of Mississippi, President, and Alexander H. Stephens, of Georgia, Vice-President of the new Confederacy. The reported vote for Davis is unanimous; but it is historically related by Stephens that Howell Cobb and Robert Toombs were also aspirants, and that Davis himself preferred the chief command of the rebel armies. For the moment, however, offices were plenty, and each of the leaders received a prominent station. Cobb remained presiding officer of the rebel Congress; Toombs became Secretary of State; and if not completely satisfied, all acquiesced in the distribution of honors. Davis was sent for and inaugurated at Montgomery, on Monday, February 18th. In his inaugural address he intimated that they would permit the non-seceded Slave States to join their confederacy; "but, beyond this," he continued, "if I mistake not the judgment and will of the people, a reunion with the States from which we have separated is neither practicable nor desirable."

If the remotest doubt remained, from previous indications and this official hint, that the whole purpose and animus of the revolt was the establishment of a powerful slaveocracy, that doubt was removed by the public declaration of Mr. Stephens, the new Vice-President. In a speech which he made at Savannah, Ga., on the 21st of March, he defined the ruling idea of the conspiracy in the following frank language:

"The prevailing ideas entertained by him (Jefferson) and most of the leading statesmen at the time of the formation of the old constitution, were that the enslavement of the African was in violation of the laws of nature; that it was wrong in principle, socially, morally, and politically. It was an evil they knew not well how to deal with; but the general opinion of that day was, that somehow or other, in the order of Providence the institution would be evanescent and pass away. This idea, though not incorporated in the Constitution, was the prevailing idea at that time. The Constitution it is true, secured every essential guarantee to the institution while it should last, and hence no argument can be justly urged against the constitutional guarantees thus secured, because of the common sentiment of the day. Those ideas, however, were fundamentally wrong. They rested upon the assumption of the equality of races. This was an error. It was a sandy foundation, and the government built upon it fell when the storm came and the wind blew. Our new government is founded upon exactly the opposite idea; its foundations are laid, its corner-stone rests, upon the great truth that the negro is not equal to the white man; that slavery, subordination to the superior race, is his natural and normal condition. This, our new government, is the first in the history of the world, based upon this great physical, philosophical, and moral truth."

Mr. Stephens was no less enthusiastic in his estimate of the material resources of the new confederacy. "We have all the essential elements of a high national career," continued he. "The idea has been given out at the North, and even in the Border States, that we are too small and too weak to maintain a separate nationality. This is a great mistake. In extent of territory we embrace 564,000 square miles and upwards. This is upwards of 200,000 square miles more than was included within the limits of the original thirteen States. It is an area of country more than double the territory of France or the Austrian Empire. France, in round numbers, has but 212,000 square miles; Austria, in round numbers, has but 248,000 square miles. Ours is greater than both combined. It is greater than all France, Spain, Portugal, and Great Britain, including England, Ireland, and Scotland together. In population we have upwards of 5,000,000, according to the census of 1860 ; this includes white and black. The entire population, including white and black, of the original Thirteen States was less than 4,000,000 in 1790, and still less in 1776, when the independence of our fathers was achieved. If they, with a less population, dared maintain their independence against the greatest power on earth, shall we have any apprehension of maintaining ours now ? "

CHAPTER IV.

LINCOLN.

From the false political principles and the perilous official neglect of the old administration—from the dissensions and impotence of Congress, and from the threatening attitude and the hostile preparations of the South, all parties and persons now turned to the President-elect and the incoming administration. During the winter many earnest but over-hasty patriots had besought him to intervene by some public declaration. But Mr. Lincoln preserved a discreet silence, though in confidential letters to responsible personal friends of opposing politics he repeated his former assertions that, while adhering tenaciously to the Republican doctrine of "No extension of slavery," he bore no ill-will to the South, meditated no aggression on her rights, and would on the contrary treat her with liberal indulgence in matters of minor controversy.

As the day of inauguration approached, various legislatures of the Free States by formal resolutions invited him to visit their capitals on his way to Washington; a call which his deep popular sympathy moved him to accept. Starting from home on the 11th of February, he accordingly passed through the principal cities between Springfield and New York, and between New York and Washington.

Unprecedented crowds came forth to see the new Chief

Magistrate. Could the quick intelligence of the American people be otherwise than intensely curious to behold this remarkable man, whose strange career they had heard outlined in the recent election speeches? His obscure birth in the deep seclusion of the Kentucky forests; how he read Weems' Life of Washington by the flickering firelight in an humble pioneer cabin in Indiana; how, as a tall emigrant-boy, he split rails to fence his father's clearing in Illinois; how, launching his solitary canoe on the Sangamon, he sought his own fortune, becoming flatboatman, postmaster, deputy county surveyor, and captain of volunteers in the Black Hawk Indian War; how, commencing with a borrowed Blackstone, he argued cases before neighborhood juries, followed itinerant Circuit Courts from county to county, and gradually became the first lawyer in his State; how in a primitive community, where politics dealt with every office from postmaster to President, he rose in public service from Representative in the Vandalia Legislature to President-elect of the nation.

The people had also heard how this elevation was tried by the touchstone of sleepless rivalry, of unscrupulous criticism, of a mighty political conflict of party and of principle. How, in the momentous slavery discussion of the day, he was the champion who had overcome Douglas, the hitherto victorious Philistine of the Kansas-Nebraska Bill; his matchless definition of the political injustice of slavery, applicable to all nations and ages: "When the white man governs himself, that is self-government; but when he governs himself and also governs another man, that is more than self-government—that is despotism;" his irrefutable statement of the natural right of every man "to eat the bread, without leave of anybody else, which his own hand earns;" his prophetic statesmanship, in declaring that "the Union cannot permanently endure half slave and half free," four months before Wm. H. Seward proclaimed the "irrepressible conflict."

So much, the newspapers, campaign documents, and stump speakers had told the country. The remainder, which his intimate Illinois neighbors could have related, the people half divined from what they heard. That he had risen from obscurity to fame, from ignorance to eloquence, from want to rulership, uncontaminated by vice, undefiled by temptation, without schools, without family influence, without wealth; championed by no clique, fraternity, or sect; clinging to no skirt of corporation, interest, or combination; conspicuous without affectation, winning popularity without art, and receiving consideration without parade; rendering his party not only every service it requested, but, by his talent, leading it from despondency to success, and from success to renown; meanwhile, at every stage of his career, walking among his fellow-men with such irreproachable personal conduct, that his very name grew into a proverb of integrity, and passed among the people of his entire State as the genuine coin-current and recognized token of social, moral, and political uprightness.

Malicious gossip and friendly jest had both, during the campaign, described the "railsplitter" candidate as possessing great personal ugliness; this was now seen to be an utter mistake. The people beheld in the new President a man six feet four inches in height, a stature which of itself would be hailed in any assemblage as one of the outward signs of leadership; joined to this was a spare but muscular frame, and large and strongly marked features corresponding to his unusual stature. Quiet in demeanor, but erect in bearing, his face even in repose was not unattractive; and when lit up by his open, genial smile, or illuminated in the utterance of a strong or stirring thought, his countenance was positively handsome. His voice, pitched in rather a high key, but of great clearness and penetration, made his public remarks audible to a wide circle of listeners. His speeches were short; but his pithy, epigrammatic sentences, full of logical directness and force, presented the questions of the hour in new and unwonted aspects, which the exhaustive discussions of the campaign had not yet reached.

It would be impossible within any short space to give an analytic summary of the twenty to thirty short addresses he delivered on this journey. But, so long as the nation shall live, every American ought to remember his thrilling key-note of that crisis, uttered in his very first speech at Indianapolis; an admonition equally valuable to statesmen or people in every emergency which the future may bring. " The people," said he, "when they rise in mass in behalf of the Union and the liberties of their country, truly may it be said, ' The gates of hell cannot prevail against them.' In all trying positions in which I shall be placed—and doubtless I shall be placed in many such—my reliance will be upon you and the people of the United States; and I wish you to remember, now and forever, that it is your business and not mine ; that if the Union of these States and the liberties of this people shall be lost, it is but little to any one man of fifty-two years of age, but a great deal to the thirty millions of people who inhabit these United States, and to their posterity in all coming time. It is your business to rise up and preserve Union and liberty for yourselves, and not for me."

For one thing Mr. Buchanan and his Cabinet should be remembered with gratitude. All winter lŏng there had been fears and rumors that the conspirators were maturing a plot to seize the capital, the public buildings, and the archives, forcibly prevent the inauguration of Lincoln, and thus make themselves the *de facto* successors of the Buchanan administration. There were indeed many threats, boasts, and warnings, to justify apprehension on this score, but an investigation held by a Committee of Congress, disclosed no traceable combination. Under such apprehension, however, Mr. Buchanan authorized General Scott to assemble sufficient troops at Washington to insure both a peaceable count of the electoral votes on February 13th, and the peaceable inauguration of the President-elect, which latter event took place with due formalities, and in the presence of great crowds, on the 4th of March, 1861.

Mr. Lincoln's inaugural address made a frank declaration of his policy on the leading points of controversy. He repeated that he had no purpose, directly or indirectly, to interfere with the institution of slavery in the States where it existed. But he also asserted that the Union is perpetual; that secession resolves or ordinances are legally void; that acts of violence, within any State or States, against the authority of the United States, are insurrectionary or revolutionary; and that to the extent of his ability he should cause the laws to be faithfully executed in all the States. The Union would defend itself, hold its property and places, and collect the duties and imposts; "but, beyond what may be necessary for these objects, there will be no invasion, no using of force against or among the people anywhere." There should be no bloodshed or violence, unless forced upon the national authority. Temporary discontent he would tolerate; the exercise of offices in disaffected districts he would forego; he would continue to furnish the mails unless repelled; he would endeavor to preserve that sense of perfect security most favorable to calm thought and renewed allegiance. An unanswerable argument against disunion and an earnest appeal to reason and lawful remedy, he followed by a most impressive declaration of peace and good-

I.—3

will: "In your hands, my dissatisfied fellow-countrymen, and not in mine, is the momentous issue of civil war. The Government will not assail you. You can have no conflict without being yourselves the aggressors. You have no oath registered in heaven to destroy the Government; while I shall have the most solemn one to preserve, protect, and defend it."

Unhappily the burden and difficulty of administration was already heavier than he or the public were aware. He had come into office sharing the general belief that Major Anderson was secure in his stronghold of Sumter until the rebel batteries should become powerful enough to drive him out. On the contrary, a subtler and more unfailing enemy than the rebels—starvation—was rapidly forcing the brave little garrison to surrender. On the morning after inauguration letters from Sumter were put into the President's hands, showing that the fort contained provisions for only a little more than a month longer, and adding the professional opinion of Anderson and his officers that a well-appointed fleet and an army of twenty thousand men would be needed to raise the siege, so formidable had the encircling rebel batteries already become.

Such a fleet and such an army were not in existence, nor could they be organized for many months. After mature consideration General Scott advised the President that it was practically impossible to relieve or reinforce Sumter, and that, as a mere military question, it was necessary to order its evacuation.

To Mr. Lincoln, who had only a few days before publicly promised the nation that he would "hold, occupy, and possess, the property and places belonging to the Government," this was indeed a trying alternative. He ordered a re-examination of the whole subject, and Cabinet, military, and

naval officers joined in its discussion. Among the plans of
relief was one urged by Captain G. V. Fox, who, even under
General Scott's adverse criticism, convinced the President
and a majority of the Cabinet that he could, by means of
open boats and small tugs, in a dark night throw a small
quantity of provisions and a few men into the fort. The political aspects of the case, however, remained still to be considered. The President, therefore, on March 15th propounded
to his Cabinet the written question, "Assuming it to be
possible to provision Fort Sumter, is it wise under all the
circumstances of the case to attempt to do so?" To this
the Cabinet made written replies, five members arguing
against the policy of attempting relief, and only two in its
favor. The majority, led by Mr. Seward, argued that any
possible relief would only be temporary, and that a disastrous
failure, and the eventual loss of the fort would produce more
damaging political results, than to give it up at once under
the imperative military necessity already existing, and for
which the new administration was in no wise responsible.

Two or three collateral questions connected themselves
with the main one. The exposed situation of Fort Pickens
had become known to Lincoln, and one of his earliest official
acts was to order its reinforcement from the fleet ; but of the
conditions of the January truce he was not informed. He was
therefore waiting in painful anxiety to receive news that his
order had been executed and Pickens reinforced, for the suc
cessful strengthening of that point would have an important
influence in deciding the question of Sumter.

Another secondary consideration was the attitude of Virginia. Rebel influences in her Legislature had ordered a
State convention, to which convention her people had elected
a large majority of professedly loyal members. Their loyalty, however, was of a qualified sort, deeply tinctured with

factional prejudice, and irritated with the imaginary wrongs
of the South. Upon this element, rebel intrigue and conspiracy were working with telling effect; and instead of declaring and practising frank and direct adherence to the
Government, the union members were fulminating baseless
complaints, demanding impossible guarantees, and pleading
indulgent excuses for the course of South Carolina and the
Cotton Republics. And this condition of misdirected and
unstable loyalty was also wide-spread among the leaders and
people of the Border States 'of Maryland, Kentucky, and
Missouri.

How to deal with such a morbid and disturbed public sentiment—how to treat this unnatural, contradictory, and half-
hearted allegiance, was a problem of direct bearing on the
Sumter question. Mr. Seward, optimist by nature, believed
and argued that the revolution throughout the South had
spent its force and was on the wane; and that the evacuation
of Sumter, and the manifestation of kindness and confidence
to the Rebel and Border States, would undermine the conspiracy, strengthen the union sentiment and union majorities, and restore allegiance and healthy political action without resort to civil war.

Mr. Lincoln shared Seward's pacific inclinations, but not
his optimism. He deferred his decision; gathered information from Anderson, from Charleston, from Richmond, waited
in anxious suspense for news from Pickens. No substantial
encouragement, however, reached him from any quarter.
Anderson had no faith in a relief expedition. All union sentiment had disappeared from South Carolina. The Virginia
Convention was evidently playing fast and loose with treason;
and finally, General Scott was so far wrought upon by the
insane cry for concession to gratify the morbid patriotism
which yet found expression in the South, that he advised

the evacuation of Pickens as well as Sumter. To crown all, news came that the commander of the fleet at Pensacola had refused to allow the reinforcement of Fort Pickens from the ships, because of Buchanan's January truce, and of the technical objection that General Scott's order had not come through the regular channels of the Navy Department.

Amid these growing difficulties and dangers Mr. Lincoln felt that the time for decisive action had arrived. On March 29th a second and final cabinet discussion was held, in which there appeared a change of sentiment. Four of his seven counsellors now voted for an attempt to relieve Anderson, and at the close of the meeting the President ordered the preparation of the expedition proposed by Captain Fox. Three ships of war, with a transport and three swift steam-tugs, a supply of open boats, provisions for six months, and two hundred recruits, were fitted out in New York with all possible secrecy, and sailed from that port, after unforeseen delays, on April 9th and 10th, under sealed orders to rendezvous before Charleston Harbor at daylight on the morning of the 11th.

Coincident with this, the President, deeming the safety of Fort Pickens no less essential than that of Sumter, at once sent new and peremptory orders to the commander of the fleet, and also ordered the secret preparation of another and separate naval expedition to still further strengthen that post. The simultaneous preparation of the two produced a certain confusion and mutual embarrassment; but the latter was got off first, and, arriving safely, increased the garrison of Fort Pickens, including those already landed from the fleet, to 858 men, with provisions for six months, thus rendering it impregnable to rebel assault.

If we may credit abundant indications, the authorities at Montgomery did not believe they would need to resort to their guns. As soon as the provisional government was organized, three rebel commissioners were appointed to proceed to Washington to negotiate for "recognition," for "adjustment of differences," and for possession of the federal forts. Two efforts to obtain Sumter by intrigue had failed; nevertheless, they still had faith a third attempt might succeed with the new administration.

Through a conspirator who still professed loyalty, they presented their application to Mr. Seward, Secretary of State. Mr. Seward answered courteously, but decidedly, that the new administration could have nothing to do either with the rebel government or its emissaries; and to a written paper sent to the State Department by the commissioners, he wrote an unofficial "memorandum" reply of the same purport. This properly finished the negotiation; but the commissioners, authorized to do so by the government they affected to represent, sought excuse to delay their departure, and Associate Justice Campbell, of the Supreme Court of the United States, volunteered to act as an unofficial intermediary in continuing to press their errand upon the Secretary of State. Campbell had at the beginning publicly opposed secession and still professed loyalty; and in that friendly and patriotic guise was admitted by the Secretary of State to an intimacy he could never have gained under his true colors. It seems that Seward, in this unofficial intimacy, did not hesitate to tell Campbell of his own willingness to give up Sumter, and of his belief that the President, upon the recommendation of General Scott, would order its evacuation. This was about the time of the first Cabinet discussion of the direct proposition, when five members voted for evacuation and only two against it, and the general situation of affairs strongly supported Mr. Seward's course of reasoning.

Whatever may have been his language, a patriot could not

have misunderstood it.   But Campbell had meanwhile become so far committed to the cause of the conspiracy, that he conveyed his information to the commissioners as a virtual pledge of the evacuation of Sumter, and they sent the news to Montgomery in high glee.

As a matter of fact, President Lincoln had not at that date decided the Sumter question ; he was following his own sagacious logic in arriving at a conclusion, which was at least partially reached on the 29th of March, when, as we have seen, he made the order to prepare the relief expedition. By this time, Campbell, in extreme impatience to further rebellion, was importuning Seward for explanation ; and Seward, finding his former prediction at fault, thought it best not to venture a new one.   Upon consultation, therefore, the President authorized him to carry to Campbell the first and only assurance the Administration ever made with regard to Sumter—namely—that he would not change the military status at Charleston without giving notice.

This, be it observed, occurred on the 1st of April, about which time the policy of Seward favoring delay and conciliation finally and formally gave way before the President's stronger self-assertion and his carefully matured purpose to force rebellion to put itself flagrantly and fatally in the wrong by attacking Fort Sumter.

CHAPTER V

SUMTER.

GOVERNOR PICKENS, of South Carolina, began about the 1st of January to build batteries to isolate and reduce Fort Sumter; and the newly made General Beauregard was on the 1st of March sent by the rebel government to Charleston to assume direction of military affairs and to complete the preparations for its capture. The Governor had been exceedingly anxious that the capture should be attempted before the expiration of Mr. Buchanan's presidential term—that is, between the 12th of February and the 4th of March. "Mr. Buchanan cannot resist," wrote the Governor to Jefferson Davis, "because he has not the power. Mr. Lincoln may not attack, because the cause of quarrel will have been, or may be considered by him, as past." But the rebel President doubtless thought it unwise to risk offending and alienating his party friends at the North by placing the responsibility of such an affront and loss upon their administration. Even when General Beauregard came, the Governor was admonished that no attack must be attempted without mature preparation, as a failure would seriously demoralize and perhaps prematurely wreck the rebellion.

Beauregard found, as he reports, that Sumter was naturally "a perfect Gibraltar," and that only the weakness of the garrison rendered its capture reasonably feasible. He therefore set himself to work, first of all, to devise obstructions and defences against expected reinforcements, and secondly, to build batteries to breach the walls. He was himself a skilful engineer; many of the works were already well advanced; there was an ample supply of guns and mortars; he had but to make requisitions to obtain unlimited slave labor to do the drudgery of ditching and raising embankments; his improvised volunteer army could give all their time to drill and artillery practice; and, most favorable of all, this work went on in certain immunity from any molestation except through the chance of a relieving expedition to come by sea. The commander was ambitious, the men were enthusiastic, and the Governor untiring in his revolutionary ardor and impatience. It is, therefore, little wonder that, after a month of laborious effort and co-operation, Beauregard telegraphed (April 1st) to Montgomery: "Batteries ready to open Wednesday or Thursday. What instructions?"

Up to this time the rebel government indulged the pleasing hope that Lincoln would give up the fort and save them the dreaded ordeal of war. Justice Campbell had ingeniously misreported the sense and purport of Seward's conversations; and the commissioners and their Washington cronies, with equally blind zeal, sent rosy despatches on the strength of exaggerated street-rumors. So confident were they of such a result that Governor Pickens, Secretary Walker, and General Beauregard found some difficulty in settling among themselves the exact conditions upon which they would permit Anderson and his garrison to depart when the order to evacuate Sumter should be sent him.

The illusion began to fade away on the 1st of April, when Commissioner Crawford telegraphed to Governor Pickens: "I am authorized to say this Government will not undertake to supply Sumter without notice to you." This language did not resemble the order for evacuation they had been impatiently expecting, and the rebel authorities at once determined to make Anderson feel the pressure of the siege. Next day, orders were issued to stop all courtesies to the garrison; to prohibit all supplies from the city; to permit no one to depart from the fort, and to establish the rigid surveillance of hostile lines.

Anderson himself, relying upon rebel rumors and Crawford's baseless despatches, appears to have made up his mind that the garrison would be withdrawn; and he expresses himself as being "greatly surprised" when on April 7th he received a confidential letter, drafted by Lincoln, but copied and signed by Cameron, under date of April 4th, informing him that a relieving expedition would be sent; requesting him to hold out, if possible, till its arrival; stating also, however, that the President desired to subject him and his command to no unusual danger or hardship beyond those common in military life, and therefore authorizing him to capitulate when in his judgment it might become necessary. One of the few faults chargeable to Anderson is that to this thoughtful and considerate instruction, framed by Lincoln himself (but which he supposed to be the language of Cameron), he replied in a petulant and ill-natured spirit, writing: "I frankly say that my heart is not in the war which I see is to be thus commenced." His subsequent gallantry, and steadfast loyalty, however, justify his countrymen in a liberal forgiveness of the passing indiscretion. It turned out curiously enough that Anderson's letter was, through a dishonorable trick of the rebels, captured by them and sent to Montgomery, where during the whole war it remained buried in the Confederate archives, and hence the offensive sentence never came to the knowledge of the kind-hearted and generous Lincoln.

Following the notice received through Crawford, the rebels were for about a week in a tantalizing fever of suspense and uncertainty. The most contradictory telegrams
came from their commissioners and secret advisers in Washington; the most perplexing and misleading rumors reached
them from New York. The war powers of the Union were
clearly enough astir; troops were moving and ships were
loading; but for what object? Was their destination Sumter or Pickens, New Orleans, or St. Domingo? Different
circumstances pointed to any or either of these places, but
the most subtle espionage failed to obtain the certain clue.

The mystery was finally solved on the evening of April 8th.
A government messenger arrived in Charleston, reported
himself to Governor Pickens, and was immediately admitted
by him to an interview at which General Beauregard was
present. The messenger read to them an official communication, drafted by President Lincoln. It ran as follows:

"I am directed by the President of the United States to
notify you to expect an attempt will be made to supply Fort
Sumter with provisions only, and that if such attempt be
not resisted, no effort to throw in provisions, arms, or ammunition will be made without further notice, or in case of
an attack upon the fort."

The next morning after this notice was read to Governor
Pickens and General Beauregard in Charleston, the main
portion of the relieving expedition, under command of Captain G. V. Fox, sailed from New York Harbor. It consisted
of the transport Baltic with the provisions and contingent
reinforcements, the war-steamers Pawnee, Pocahontas, Har-
riet Lane, and the steam-tugs Uncle Ben, Yankee, and Free-
born. The fleet had orders to rendezvous ten miles east of
Charleston Harbor on the morning of April 11th. The instructions to Captain Fox were short, but explicit: "You will

take charge," wrote the Secretary of War, " of the transports
in New York, having the troops and supplies on board, and
endeavor in the first instance to deliver the subsistence.   If
you are opposed in this, you are directed to report the fact
to the senior naval officer of the harbor, who will be instructed by the Secretary of the Navy to use his entire force
to open a passage, when you will, if possible, effect an entrance, and place both troops and supplies in Fort Sumter."

Lincoln's notice having been communicated to the Confederate authorities in Montgomery, Jefferson Davis and his
compeers in revolution resolved to begin the war without
further delay.   To permit provisions to be sent to Anderson,
after three months of battery-building, would jeopardize the
confidence and adhesion of the ultra fire-eaters, and suffer
the insurrection to collapse.   The notice was received on
the evening of April 8th; next day, the 9th, appears to have
been spent in deliberation and in verifying the situation by
inquiries from the rebel commissioners in Washington; on
the 10th, Beauregard was instructed to demand the evacuation of Sumter, and, in case of refusal, to reduce it.   At two
o'clock in the afternoon of the following day (April 11th), he
sent two of his aids to make the demand, in answer to which
Anderson, with the unanimous concurrence of his officers,
wrote a prompt refusal.   The occasion seems to have called
out some general conversation, in the course of which Anderson said to the aids: "I will await the first shot, and if
you do not batter us to pieces, we will be starved out in a
few days."   The remark repeated to Beauregard and to
Montgomery, caused the impression that Anderson desired
to capitulate, and another message was sent him, offering to
permit him to do so at his own convenience, if he would
designate the time, and agree in the meanwhile not to use
his guns against the rebels unless they should fire on Sum-

ter. Anderson was shrewd enough to see that this would leave their guns free to beat back the fleet, and shaped his reply accordingly. He stated that he would evacuate the fort by noon on the 15th of April, "and that I will not, in the meantime, open my fires upon your forces, unless compelled to do so by some hostile act against this fort or the flag of my Government, by the forces under your command, or some portion of them, or by the perpetration of some act showing a hostile intention on your part against this fort or the flag it bears, should I not receive, prior to that time, controlling instructions from my Government, or additional supplies." This reply was, of course, unsatisfactory to the rebels.

The interchange of these several messages had consumed the afternoon and night of April 11th, and at 3:20 A.M., of the morning of April 12th, Beauregard's aids handed Anderson a note stating that he would open fire upon Sumter in one hour from that time.

The inhabitants of Charleston had now for more than three months followed the development of secession and rebellion with unflagging zeal and daily interest, until they began to regard the affairs of Sumter as their own pet and exclusive drama. It had afforded them excitement upon excitement—speeches, meetings, drills, parades, flag-raisings, bonfires, salutes, music, and banners; reaching into their social and family life, it had carried their fathers, sons, brothers, and friends away into the camps and trenches. Sumter had been their daily talk and nightly dream; and this interest grew into a morbid curiosity as the drama approached its long-predicted climax. There had been little or no effort to conceal the changing aspects of preparations and orders during the last few days; and, as a result, the general populace of the city became informed, almost as well

as the officers, of the precise hour when the bombardment
would begin.   In the gray and yet uncertain twilight of this
April morning, therefore, the Charlestonians of all ages and
sexes came thronging down the streets to the wharves of the
city, to find favorable locations for viewing the coming spec-
tacle, in something of the spirit in which Rome of the
Cæsars crowded to the Coliseum to witness the savage and
sanguinary combats of the arena.

At half-past four o'clock, on the morning of April 12th,
1861, while yet the lingering night lay upon the waters of
the bay, leaving even the outline of Fort Sumter scarcely
discernible, the assembled spectators saw a flash from the
mortar battery near old Fort Johnson, on the south side of
the harbor, and an instant after a bombshell rose in a slow,
high curve through the air, and fell upon the fort.   To the
beholders it was the inauguration of the final scene in their
local drama; to the nation and world at large, it began a
conflict of such gigantic proportions and far-reaching conse-
quence, that it will forever stand as one of the boldest land-
marks in history.   Gun after gun responded to the signal,
until, in the course of another hour, all the encircling rebel
batteries were in the heat and activity of a general bombardment.

Universal wonder was created at the time, and continued
curiosity has been excited since, by the fact that this bombardment, ending in the surrender of the fort, should have
continued for the space of thirty-six hours without the loss
of a single life in the besieged garrison.   The apparent mystery is easily enough understood when we come to study
and comprehend the exact conditions and course of the
fight.

Fort Sumter was a work dating from comparatively recent
times, built of brick upon an artificial island formed in the

shallows nearly midway at the entrance of Charleston harbor. It was a five-sided structure, about three hundred by three hundred and fifty feet in size; its walls were some eight feet thick and forty feet high. It was capable of mounting one hundred and forty guns, two tiers in casemates and one behind the parapet. When Anderson took possession of it the preceding Christmas, the casemates were in an unfinished condition, and only a few guns were mounted. Captain Foster, the accomplished engineer of the fort, had, however, since then, by the many expedients known to military science, and by help of a considerable force of workmen and laborers, pushed its defences forward to a state of relative completeness, even with the limited means and materials within the fort. Most of the embrasures of the lower tier of casemates were closed. A total armament of forty-eight guns was ready for use. Of these twenty-one were in the casemates, and twenty-seven on the rampart, *en barbette*. The garrison consisted of nine commissioned officers, sixty-eight non-commissioned officers and privates, eight musicians, and forty-three non-combatant workmen, to whom, during the last ten days, the besiegers had refused permission to depart, in order that they might help consume Anderson's small stock of provisions, and thus hasten the process of reducing the fort by starvation.

The rebels had built their siege-works on the approaching points of the islands forming the harbor. These lay in a sort of triangle about the fort: Sullivan's Island, containing Fort Moultrie, to the northeast at a distance of 1,800 yards; Cumming's Point, on Morris Island, to the south at a distance of 1,300 yards; and on James Island, near old Fort Johnson, to the west at a distance of 2,500 yards. Their total armament embraced forty-seven guns.

Thus, in numbers, the armaments appeared about equal,

but the existing conditions created an immense disparity. Anderson's fire was diffused; the rebel fire was concentrated. Anderson's barbette guns, more than half his pieces, were exposed; most of the rebel guns were sheltered in bomb-proofs of palmetto logs and sand; some protected with sloping roofs of railroad iron. Anderson had only a garrison of 128 souls all told; while a volunteer force of from four to six thousand supported the rebel batteries. The greatest difference, however, was in the quality of the ordnance. Anderson's guns could only deliver a horizontal fire against the besiegers' earth-walls and bomb-proofs. But seventeen of the rebel pieces were mortars, delivering what is termed a vertical fire; that is, throwing their bursting shells by means of a high curve through the air, so as to drop down upon the parapet and inside the walls of the besieged fort.

The garrison of Sumter, notwithstanding its tedious confinement, was in excellent spirit, and, since the long apprehended contest had finally come, was quite ready to make a manful resistance. Even the forty-three non-combatant workmen caught the impulse of fight and freely volunteered their help. The needful preparations had been already made, and since the 10th every one had by order changed his quarters into the gun casemates. Here they were securely housed when at 4.30 A.M. the rebel cannonade began. It was not yet daylight, and for some hours the fort made no reply, but lay in the morning twilight as silent and apparently as unconcerned as if it were tenantless. The rations had already become uncomfortably short; the last barrel of flour was issued two or three days before, and now there was little left to subsist upon except pork and water. On this mainly the command made a breakfast, and at about seven o'clock Captain Abner Doubleday fired the first gun from the fort at an iron-clad battery on Cumming's Point.

Reliefs were stationed at other guns, and soon Sumter was sending back a spirited reply.

The three hours of unopposed bombardment from the rebel batteries had by this time already determined one important phase of the fight. Carefully watching the effect of the enemy's cannonade, it was apparent, without further question, that under the concentrated missiles of their guns, and particularly because of the precision of their vertical fire, it would be folly to expose the gunners on the rampart or the open parade of the fort. Had Sumter contained a full war garrison, new men could have replaced those killed or disabled; but, with his slender force, Anderson decided that he could not afford this risk, and therefore at once ordered an abandonment of all the barbette guns and a few mounted on the parade to throw shells, restricting the men rigidly to the casemates. Thus at one swoop his fighting armament was reduced more than one-half. This, however, was not the worst; it practically annihilated the offensive strength of the fort. Of the twenty-one casemate guns but four were forty-two pounders, the rest only thirty-twos, a weight of metal of little avail against the enemy's strong earthworks and iron roofs.

In this way the cannonade went actively on during the forenoon of April 12th, without much damage or effect, except upon the buildings in both Sumter and Moultrie, ordinarily occupied as barracks and quarters. Sumter suffered most in this respect: the balls striking the face of its walls merely buried themselves in the brick-work, without passing through; but those which nearly or quite grazed the parapet, in their fall took the buildings or wall in reverse, coming as they did from three sides. The men, however, while sheltered in casemates, were beyond the reach of these missiles. So too of the bombs. Falling on the parapet and the

5

open parade of Sumter and exploding, their destructive force spent itself upon mere inanimate material.

About noon Anderson's men found they had been working with too much ardor; that their stock of 700 cartridges would soon be exhausted. They set themselves to work to remedy this deficiency, though with small speed, for they had only six needles in the fort with which to sew up cartridge-bags.

Toward one o'clock a new hope cheered them; they saw two ships, and soon after a third, bearing the stars and stripes, appear off the harbor; it was a part of the relieving expedition they had been warned to expect. Unfortunately, it proved unable to succor the fort either on that or the succeeding day. Through a confusion of orders, the flagship of the squadron with its commanding officer, and the instructions for this emergency, and having on board also the sailors who were required to man the boats to carry the supplies and soldiers to Sumter, had been detached from this duty and sent to the Gulf of Mexico. A severe storm delayed some of the vessels, and prevented the tugs from reaching the harbor; and this storm also prevented the officers from making use of the limited resources remaining. Therefore, to their chagrin, they and their men were forced by these untoward circumstances, and through no neglect of their own, to remain for twenty-four hours little else than spectators of the bombardment to its close.

During the afternoon of the first day Sumter kept up its fire, though with greatly slackened speed. Only six guns were kept in action for the remainder of the day: two against Cumming's Point on the south, and four against Fort Moultrie and other batteries on Sullivan's Island to the north. At nightfall even these ceased, as also did most of the guns in the rebel batteries; their mortars, however, keeping up a sullen and steady discharge of bombs upon the fort at intervals of about ten minutes, the whole of the dark and stormy night which followed.

On the morning of the second day, April 13th, the rebels began their general cannonade with both increased vigor and increased precision; to which the garrison, after its breakfast of pork and water, and having somewhat replenished its stock of cartridges, again made a "spiteful" reply. It is impossible to estimate how long this mere interchange of shot and shell might have continued, had not other elements intervened to bring the combat to a close.

On three of the five sides of Sumter, just inside the walls, stood long and substantial buildings used as barracks, officers' quarters, and for other purposes. These had been several times set on fire by hot shot during the first day, though as often readily extinguished by the garrison. The rebels had not failed to notice the effect; and on the second morning their use of these missiles became more frequent. About nine o'clock of the second day these buildings were once more in a blaze, and this time the fire caught in a portion of the roof of the officers' quarters which it was not immediately possible for the men to reach. The flames were quickly beyond control; and now the serious problem was to remove as much powder from the magazine as might be needed for use, before that proceeding should become impossible. Fifty barrels were thus obtained and distributed about the casemates, when it was necessary to close and secure the door of the magazine.

Thus, by noon of the second day, the inmates of the fort were exposed, not alone to the peril of the enemy's shot and shell, but also to the immediate discomfort and danger of a serious conflagration. Within the limited area of the fort the heat became intense; the air was filled with floating cinders; and, blown downward by the current of the seabreeze, a stifling, blinding smoke finally drove the men into the casemates, and even to these retreats the floating fire-flakes pursued them. The situation became too dangerous to keep the fifty barrels of powder rescued from the maga-zine; by order of Anderson, all but five were rolled out of the embrasures into the sea.

About one o'clock the flagstaff of the fort was shot away, having been hit a number of times previously; and, although the flag was soon after again raised on a jury-mast on the parapet, the clouds of smoke concealed it from the rebel view. Seeing the great conflagration, the disappearance of the flag, and a total cessation of fire from Sumter's guns, they not unreasonably concluded that the garrison was ready to surrender. The eccentric Senator Wigfall, doing duty as a volunteer aid on one of the islands, was sent by a subordinate officer to ascertain the fact; and, being brought before the commander, with more grandiloquence than au-thority, offered to permit Anderson to name his own terms of evacuation. Anderson replied that he would accept the terms offered him by Beauregard at the time of his first summons, on the 11th. Wigfall thereupon returned to his post, where, in turn, with more enthusiasm than memory, he reported an unconditional surrender. Meanwhile, three aids arrived direct from Beauregard, with an offer of assistance to extinguish the flames, and the misunderstanding became apparent. Anderson, in some anger, was disposed to renew his fight; upon suggestion of the aids, however, he waited till the blunder could be referred to Beauregard. This commander reconciled all difficulty by agreeing to Anderson's proposal; and at noon of the following day, Sunday, April 14, 1861, the faithful commander and his faithful garrison, with an impres-sive ceremony of prayer and salute, hauled down the flag of the United States, and evacuated Fort Sumter.

CHAPTER VI.

THE CALL TO ARMS.

THE assault upon Fort Sumter had doubtless been ordered by the rebel government under the hope, if not the belief, that it would not provoke immediate or widespread civil war. It is probable that they anticipated it would bring on military movements and measures of a local and defensive character; but neither the size of the Federal army, nor the very limited war organization set on foot by the rebel congress, pointed as yet to hostilities on an extended scale. The South well knew that the frontier could not be entirely stripped of regulars; they assumed, or so pretended, that existing laws authorized no call of the militia; and, judging from the neglect of Congress, at its recent session, to pass a force bill, they might reasonably infer that it would be difficult for the new administration to obtain coercive legislation. Most of all, however, they relied upon a friendly feeling toward the South from their late Democratic party allies. Throughout the last presidential election, Northern Democrats had magnified Southern complaints as insufferable grievances, and predicted the coming revolution as a terror to obstinate voters. President Buchanan even went so far in his annual message as to assert that a neglect of Northern States to repeal their personal liberty laws would justify the South in revolutionary resistance. The newspaper press was full of kindred echoes. Potent public voices had declared that the North would not entertain— nay, would not permit, a policy of subjugation. Ex-President Franklin Pierce—Buchanan's predecessor—had given Jefferson Davis very broad confidential assurances on this head. "Without discussing the question of right," wrote he, January 6, 1860, "of abstract power to secede, I have never believed that actual disruption of the Union can occur without blood; and if, through the madness of Northern Abolitionism, that dire calamity must come, the fighting will not be along Mason's and Dixon's line merely. It [will] be within our own borders, in our own streets, between the two classes of citizens to whom I have referred. Those who defy law and scout constitutional obligations will, if we ever reach the arbitrament of arms, find occupation enough at home."

As the oracle of another faction, Douglas had made an elaborate argument in the Senate to show that the President possessed no right of coercion; repeating the theory of Buchanan's message, that the army and navy and the militia of the States could not move except behind a marshal with his writ, and that both the tongue and the arms of justice were dead in South Carolina. Similar encouragement came from many individuals of lesser note. It even appeared that the spirit of secession was finding a lodgment in the North. A member had declared on the floor of Congress that the Empire State would set up her own separate sovereignty; while in a still more radical ambition the Mayor of New York City, in an official message, proposed the secession of that metropolis, and its assumption of territorial independence as a "free city." The firing on the Star of the West, in January, had in a slight degree touched the national pride, and somewhat checked the gathering current of seditious utterance;

but there was no lack of cliques and coteries in the great cities of the North who secretly nursed plots and projects contingent on possible insurrectionary commotions and chances. One of the rebel commissioners to Washington, in the interim during which Justice Campbell relieved them of their labors of diplomatic intrigue, visited New York, where he was waited upon by the spokesman of one of these Northern cabals, who poured into the ears of his credulous listener the recital of a most marvellous scheme of local conspiracy. Two hundred of New York's best citizens, he said, were at that moment elaborating a plan to secede from both the Union and the State, seize the navy yard at Brooklyn, and the forts in the harbor, and declare New York a free city. The informant was perhaps an adventurer anxious to pocket a liberal subsidy; yet, as an echo of Mayor Wood's official proposition, the incident was not without its significance, and the eager commissioner repeated the tale by letter to Jefferson Davis, countersigned by his own personal faith that there was "something in it."

Jefferson Davis was by far too shrewd a leader to look for a literal fulfilment of any of these extravagant predictions or projects; but they afforded him a substantial basis for the belief that this class of sentiment would at least oppose and thwart the new administration in any quick or extended measures to suppress the "confederate" revolt.

On the part of the North, also, there had been grave misapprehension of the actual state of Southern opinion. For ten years the Southern threats of disunion had been empty bluster. The half-disclosed conspiracy of 1856 did not seem to extend beyond a few notorious agitators. The more serious revolutionary signs of the last three months—the retirement of Southern members from Congress, the secession of States, the seizure of federal forts and the formation of the Montgomery provisional government—were not realized in their full force by the North, because of the general confusion of politics, the rush and hurry of events, the delusive hopes of compromise held out by Congressional committees and factions, and the high-sounding professions of the Washington peace conference. More potent than all was the underlying disbelief of the North that the people at large in the South felt the stress of any real grievance. The loss of slave runaways was their most tangible accusation. Would that evil be cured by moving the Canada line down to the Ohio? If separate nationality was the object, could ten millions overcome twenty millions?—could precarious Southern credit cope with the solid accumulations of Northern capital?—could a monotonous Southern agriculture try expedients with the famous mechanical skill of the Free States?—could cotton crops feed armies like the great corn, wheat, hay, pork, and cattle regions?—and finally, would the great West permit a foreign flag to close or cover the mouth of the Mississippi? The bare suggestion seemed, and was, nonsense. They indeed saw clearly enough the ambition, treachery, and desperation of certain Southern leaders; but the North did not believe that these leaders could, in Yancey's language, "precipitate the Cotton States into a revolution"; that passing chagrin over a lost election could goad the whole Southern people, without substantial cause, into the horror and ruin of a hopeless civil war.

The firing on Sumter cleared up the political atmosphere as if by magic. The roar of Beauregard's guns changed incredulity into fact. There was no longer room for doubt. This was no mere *emeute*. Seven seceding States, with their machinery of local government and the crazy zeal of an inflamed reaction, stood behind the guns. The cool deliberation of the assault betokened plan, purpose, and confidence. The conspiracy had given way to revolution.

The news of the assault on Sumter reached Washington on Saturday, April 13th; on Sunday morning, the 14th, the President and Cabinet were met to discuss the surrender and evacuation. Sunday, though it was, Lincoln with his own hand immediately drafted the following proclamation, which was dated, issued, telegraphed, and published to the whole country on Monday morning, April 15th.

"PROCLAMATION

" BY THE PRESIDENT OF THE UNITED STATES.

"*Whereas*, the laws of the United States have been for some time past and now are opposed, and the execution thereof obstructed in the States of South Carolina, Georgia, Alabama, Florida, Mississippi, Louisiana, and Texas, by combinations too powerful to be suppressed by the ordinary course of judicial proceedings, or by the powers vested in the marshals by law : now therefore, I, ABRAHAM LINCOLN, President of the United States, in virtue of the power in me vested by the Constitution and the laws, have thought fit to call forth, and hereby do call forth the militia of the several States of the Union, to the aggregate number of seventy-five thousand, in order to suppress said combinations and to cause the laws to be duly executed.

" The details for this object will be immediately communicated to the State authorities through the War Department. I appeal to all loyal citizens to favor, facilitate, and aid this effort to maintain the honor, the integrity, and existence of our National Union, and the perpetuity of popular government, and to redress wrongs already long enough endured. I deem it proper to say that the first service assigned to the forces hereby called forth will probably be to repossess the forts, places, and property which have been seized from the Union ; and in every event the utmost care will be observed, consistently with the objects aforesaid, to avoid any devastation, any destruction of, or inter-

I.—4

ference with property, or any disturbance of peaceful citizens in any part of the country; and I hereby command the persons composing the combinations aforesaid to disperse and retire peaceably to their respective abodes within twenty days from this date.

"Deeming that the present condition of public affairs presents an extraordinary occasion, I do hereby, in virtue of the power in me vested by the Constitution, convene both Houses of Congress. Senators and Representatives are therefore summoned to assemble at their respective chambers at twelve o'clock, noon, on Thursday, the fourth day of July next, then and there to consider and determine such measures as, in their wisdom, the public safety and interest may seem to demand.

"In witness whereof, I have hereunto set my hand and caused the seal of the United States to be affixed.

"Done at the City of Washington, this fifteenth day of April, in the year of our Lord one thousand eight hundred and sixty-one, and of the independence of the United States the eighty-fifth.

"ABRAHAM LINCOLN.

"By the President.

"WILLIAM H. SEWARD, *Secretary of State.*"

The possible contingency foreshadowed by Lincoln in his Trenton address had come; and he not only redeemed his promise to "put the foot down firmly," but he took care to place it on a solid foundation. Nominally the call of the militia was based on the Act of 1795. But the broad language of the proclamation was an "appeal to all loyal citizens to favor, facilitate, and aid this effort to maintain the honor, the integrity, and existence of our National Union, and the perpetuity of popular government." The President had taken care to so shape the issue—so to strip it of all provocation or ingenious excuse, as to show the reckless malignity of the rebellion in showering red-hot shot on a starving garrison; he now asked the people to maintain their assaulted dignity and outraged authority; touching not merely the machinery of forms and statutes, but invoking directly that spirit of free government to preserve itself, against which in his opinion "the gates of hell" could not prevail.

The correctness of his faith was equal to the wisdom of his policy; for now there was seen one of those mighty manifestations of national will and national strength that mark the grand epochs of civilized history. The whole country seemed to awaken as from the trouble of a feverish dream, and once again men entered upon a conscious recognition of their proper relations to the Government. Cross-purpose and perplexed counsel faded from the public mind. Parties vanished from politics. Universal opinion recognized but two rallying-points—the camps of the South which gathered to assail the Union, and the armies of the North that rose to defend it.

From every Governor of the Free States came a prompt response of readiness to furnish to the President the desired quota of militia. In almost every county of the North was begun the enlistment of volunteers. Meetings, speeches, and parades voiced the public exhortation to patriotism. Flags and badges symbolized an eager and universal loyalty. Munificent individual donations, and subscriptions, and liberal appropriations from State Legislatures and municipal councils, poured forth lavish contributions to arm, clothe, and equip the recruits. More than double the number of men required tendered their service. Before the lapse of forty-eight hours, armed companies and regiments of volunteers were in motion toward the expected border of conflict. Public opinion became intolerant of dissent and cavil; in many instances tumultuous mobs silenced or destroyed newspapers which had ventured to print disloyal or treasonable language. There was not the slightest sign or movement of the predicted division of Northern sentiment. New York joyfully ranged herself under the flag in a monster meeting of two hundred thousand of her people. Before the surging crowds that filled the streets, and drowned all noises in their huzzas for the Union, the *New York Herald* displayed the stars and stripes, and changed its editorials from a tone of sneering lament to a fierce and incessant war-cry. Every prominent individual in the whole North was called or came voluntarily to prompt espousal of the Union cause by public letter or speech. Ex-President Buchanan, ex-President Pierce, Edward Everett, General Cass, Archbishop Hughes, Mayor Fernando Wood, John A. Dix, Wendell Phillips, Robert J. Walker, Wm. M. Evarts, Edward D. Baker, David Dudley Field, John J. Crittenden, Caleb Cushing, Hannibal Hamlin, Democrats and Republicans, conservatives and radicals, natives and foreigners, Catholics and Protestants, Maine and Oregon, all uttered a common call to their countrymen to come to the defence of the Constitution, the Government, and the Union. Of all these recognized public leaders, however, the most energetic and powerful, next to Lincoln, was Stephen A. Douglas, who in the late election had received 1,128,049 Northern votes, and 163,525 Southern votes for President. As already mentioned, he had, in a bold Senate speech, announced himself as opposed to a policy of coercion. But the wanton bombardment of Sumter exhausted his party patience, and stirred his patriotic blood to fresher and healthier impulses. On Sunday, April 14th, when the proclamation had not yet been many hours written and signed, he sought his life-long political antagonist, Abraham Lincoln, now President of the United States, and, in a long, confidential interview, assured him of his readiness to join him in unrelenting warfare against rebellion. The next morning's telegraphic despatches gave the country an authorized notice of the patriotic alliance. In a few days he started to his home in Illi-

nois; and everywhere on his journey, and until his sudden
death a few weeks later, he scarcely ceased his eloquent appeal to his fellow-citizens to rise in vindication of good
faith, of system, of order in government; declaring, with sen-
tentious vigor, "every man must be for the United States or
against it; there can be no neutrals in this war—only patriots and traitors."

Such was the grand uprising of the North. The South,
already for three months past in the turmoil of insurrection,
was once more quickened to a new activity in her fatal enterprise. She felt that the assault on Sumter was her final cast
of the die. Her people are proud and impetuous, stronger
in physical than in moral courage, more prone to daring in
behalf of error than of suffering to sustain truth. This quality was shrewdly recognized by one of the conspirators when
he gave his hesitating confederates the brutal watchword:
"You must sprinkle blood in the faces of the people."
Sumter was a bloodless conquest, but it nevertheless filled
the South with the intoxication of combat. All sentiment
adverse to secession and Southern independence had long
since disappeared under the repression of a despotic public
opinion; but now the fervor of a fanatical crusade transfused
the whole Southern population; and their motley array of
palmetto banners, rattlesnake flags, and almost as eccentric
varieties of "stars and bars," became, in their wild political
lunacy, the symbols of a holy deliverance.

The Sumter bombardment, Lincoln's proclamation, and
the enthusiastic war-spirit of the North, left the Confederate authorities at Montgomery no further hope of obtaining
peaceable separation by diplomacy or intrigue. In their
scheme of independence, while counting, with much greater
accuracy than outsiders, upon the latent military resources
of the South, they nevertheless seem to have based their

ultimate reliance upon foreign intervention in their behalf. "Cotton is king," they argued; Europe cannot exist without it; therefore, when American civil war locks up that daily food of European looms, and takes the means of earning daily bread from foreign labor, dividends from foreign capital, and activity from foreign commerce, European governments must open our ports by recognizing and protecting our flag, especially if, in addition to their needed manufacturing staple, we tempt them with the commercial harvest of free trade.

As the entering wedge to this policy, Jefferson Davis, on the 17th of April, issued his proclamation, offering letters of marque and reprisal, "under the seal of these Confederate States," to armed privateers of any nation. The commercial classes of England had, since the secession of South Carolina, manifested a strong sympathy for the rebellion, and he doubtless expected that the seas would soon swarm with predatory adventurers under shelter of the "stars and bars." A few vessels of this character did, in the subsequent years of the war, inflict incalculable damage upon shipping sailing under the Federal flag; but the extravagant scheme, of which this privateering proclamation was the key-note, withered in an early blight. Two days after its appearance President Lincoln issued a counter-proclamation, instituting a rigid blockade of the insurgent ports, and threatening that Jefferson Davis' privateers should be "held amenable to the laws of the United States for the prevention and punishment of piracy"—a warning which, from motives of public policy and the humane personal instincts of the President, was not literally enforced. The unexampled increase of the United States Navy, the extraordinary efficiency of the blockade, the vigilant foreign diplomatic service of the administration, and, above all, its vigorous prosecution of the war, left foreign powers no sufficient excuse, and overawed all passing temptations to intervene. And when the hour of distress and trial finally came to the industrial classes of England, the noble devotion of the Manchester cotton operatives to universal liberty put to shame and impotence the greedy cupidity of the cotton merchants of Liverpool.

In addition to the six or seven thousand rebel troops assembled at Charleston to aid in the reduction of Sumter, and the four or five thousand sent to Pensacola to undertake the capture of Fort Pickens, Jefferson Davis' Secretary of War had, in anticipation of the results of the bombardment, on the 8th of April called upon the seceded States for a contingent of 20,000, to which there was again, on the 16th of April, added a further call of 34,000 volunteers. In seizing the Southern arsenals the seceded States had become possessed of over one hundred thousand "serviceable" arms; at least thirty thousand others had been secured by purchase from Secretary Floyd. The arsenals also contained considerable quantities of military equipments. A variety of military stores were among the property surrendered by Twiggs in Texas; the seaboard forts, particularly those in Charleston Harbor, furnished a supply of heavy guns. Southern recruits were abundant; and out of these ready materials the Montgomery authorities proceeded as rapidly as possible, with the assistance of many skilful officers resigned or deserted from the Federal service, to improvise an army. Diplomatic agents were sent in haste to European courts. Measures were taken to thoroughly fortify the coast; permission was sought from the neighboring States to blockade the Mississippi River as high as Vicksburg and Memphis. The Confederate Congress was convened in special session; and on April 29th Jefferson Davis sent them his message, announcing that he had " in the field, at Charleston, Pensacola, Forts Morgan, Jackson, St. Philip, and Pulaski, nineteen thousand men, and sixteen thousand are now en route for Virginia." Also, that he further proposed "to organize and hold in readiness for instant action," an army of one hundred thousand men.

Between the fall of Sumter, however, and the date of this message, the whole revolution had undergone a remarkably rapid development, which essentially changed the scope and character of the contest. Hitherto the Border Slave States, as they were called—Maryland, Virginia, North Carolina, Tennessee, Kentucky, Arkansas, and Missouri—though from the beginning also deeply agitated, had taken no decisive action. Their people were divided in sympathy and interest; they favored slavery, but they also loved the Union. Every expression through a popular vote indicated strongly preponderant loyalty; but with one exception their State officials were already secretly leagued with the secession conspirators. Upon them, too, the bombardment of Sumter fell like a sudden touchstone. The proclamation of President Lincoln, and the requisition of the Secretary of War for their quota of Union volunteers, left them no further chance of concealment. Compelled to take sides, their various governors replied to the call in an insulting and contumacious refusal. From that time forward Virginia, North Carolina, Tennessee, and Arkansas were practically part and parcel of the rebellion, though some of these did not immediately make a pretence of formal adhesion by ordinances or military leagues. It would be both tedious and needless to detail the various steps and phases of their seeming revolt; it is a record of bold conspiracy, shameless usurpation, and despotic military domination, made possible by the sudden rush of popular excitement and passion consequent upon the fall of Sumter. The three others, Maryland, Kentucky, and Missouri, and also the western half of Virginia, were eventually saved to the Union, partly by the inherent loyalty of their people, partly by the quick and sustaining presence of the Union forces.

By these adhesions the revolution at a single bound augmented its area almost one-half, and nearly doubled its supporting population, its material resources, its claim to the serious attention of foreign nations. Its chiefs and leaders were, of course, correspondingly elated and hopeful. With a territory nearly four times as large as France; with five and a half millions of whites, and three and a half millions of blacks; producing by her agriculture a single staple, cotton, valued at two hundred million dollars annually; with a greatly diversified climate; with a long sea-coast, with several important harbors and many navigable rivers; with mountains, with mines, with forests containing the most valuable ship-timber in the world; with a greater variety of field and garden products than usually falls to the lot of a single people—they believed that they possessed the substantial elements of a homogeneous, prosperous, and powerful nation.

6

CHAPTER VII.

BALTIMORE.

Of all the Border Slave States, Virginia held the most equivocal and deceptive attitude. Beyond all doubt a majority of her people desired to adhere to the Union, and at an election for members of a State convention held in February the majority of professedly Union men chosen was as three to one. But when this convention met, it appeared that many of these so-called Unionists had trifled with their constituents, and finally betrayed their trust; they were Unionists only upon conditions to which the Union would never consent. Governor Letcher, of Virginia, also labored in secret activity to promote secession. There was a pestiferous clique of radical disunionists about Richmond, and, under an outward show of qualified loyalty, the conspiracy was almost as busy and as potent in the "Old Dominion" as in the Cotton States themselves. When Sumter fell, all this hidden intrigue blazed out into open insurrection. The convention, notwithstanding many previous contrary votes, held a secret session on April 17th, and passed an ordinance of secession, eighty-eight to fifty-five. The gradual but systematic arming of the State militia had been going on for a year past. Governor Letcher insultingly refused the President's call for troops on the 16th, and immediately set military expeditions in movement to seize the United States

Navy Yard at Norfolk, and the United States Armory at Harper's Ferry. The convention made a pretence of submitting the question of secession to a popular vote, to be taken on May 23d following; and then, as if in mockery, entered at once into a secret military league with the "Confederate States" on April 24th, placing Jefferson Davis in control of all her armies and military affairs, and filling the State with "foreign" regiments from the South.

In the Border State of Maryland the situation was somewhat different. The Unionists were also in the majority, with an active and influential minority for secession. Here, as elsewhere, conspiracy had been at work for months, and gained many of the prominent leaders in politics. The Legislature was believed to be unreliable. Treason had so far taken a foothold in the populous city of Baltimore, that a secret recruiting office was sending enlisted men to Charleston. But all local demonstration was as yet baffled by the unwavering loyalty of the Governor of Maryland, Thomas Holliday Hicks. He had refused and resisted all the subtle temptations and schemes of the traitors, especially in declining to call the Legislature together to give disunion the cloak of a legal starting-point.

To understand correctly the series of sudden and startling events which now occurred in quick succession, it is necessary to bear in mind that the ten miles square of Federal territory known as the District of Columbia, in which the capital of the country, Washington, is situated, lies between Virginia and Maryland, and was formed out of the original territory of those States.

In all wars, foreign or domestic, the safety of the capital, its buildings, archives, and officers, is, of course, a constant and a paramount necessity. To guard the City of Washington against a rumored plot of seizure by the conspirators,

President Buchanan had in January permitted Secretary Holt and General Scott to concentrate a small number of regular troops in it. Some of these had ever since remained there. As soon as President Lincoln decided to send provisions to Sumter, he had, in anticipation of coming dangers, ordered General Scott to take additional measures for the security of the capital, and to that end authorized him to muster into the service of the United States about fifteen companies of District militia. When Sumter fell and the proclamation was issued, as a still further precaution the first few regiments were ordered directly to Washington.

To the Massachusetts Sixth belongs the unfading honor of being the first regiment, armed and equipped for service, to respond to the President's call. Mustering on Boston Common, on Tuesday morning, April 16th, it embarked on railroad cars on Wednesday evening, April 17th, and, after a continuous popular ovation along the route, it reached Philadelphia Thursday evening, April 18th. Friday, April 19th, was the anniversary of the battle of Lexington, famous in American history. Early that morning, after a short bivouac, the regiment was once more on its way. It had been warned of danger in Baltimore; the unruly populace was excited by a series of secession meetings; part of an unarmed Pennsylvania regiment had, in its transit, been hooted and stoned the evening before. As the train approached the city, Colonel Jones, commanding the Sixth, ordered his men to load and cap their rifles, and instructed them to pay no attention to insults or even ordinary missiles, but to vigorously return any attack with firearms.

A misunderstanding existed about the method of proceeding. Colonel Jones expected that his regiment would march in a body through the open streets, and had made his dispositions accordingly. When, therefore, the train halted, he was surprised and disconcerted to find that the cars were suddenly detached from the train and from each other, and, with the troops still in them, were rapidly drawn by horses through the streets on a track running from the Philadelphia depot to the Washington depot, the two being about a mile apart. Himself and the regimental officers were in the first car; others followed, and, until eight cars had thus passed, no detention or demonstration occurred. But an excited

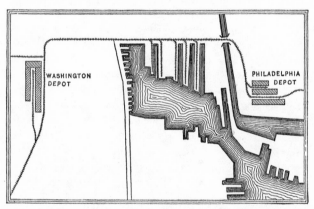

Route of the Massachusetts Sixth through Baltimore.

crowd meanwhile gathered along the track; the ninth car was received with hootings and insults, was detained by slight obstructions, and, before it finally reached the Washington depot, its windows were smashed by stones and bricks, and some of its occupants wounded by gun- and pistol-shots, the soldiers having also returned the scattering fire.

By this time the crowd, grown to formidable proportions, and fully maddened, succeeded in placing more permanent obstructions on the track—sand, paving-stones, heavy anchors from a wharf near by, and in one place had partially torn up a small bridge. Four companies still remained behind; and these were now notified by the railroad employees of the dangers ahead, and the impossibility of proceeding in the cars as the preceding companies had done. The officers thereupon consulted together, and determined to undertake the trip on foot; and, placing Captain Follansbee in command, they descended from their cars, formed deliberately on the sidewalk, and started forward.

Almost at the outset they encountered an improvised procession of the mob following a secession flag, and in an instant there was a quick and short *mêlée*. Disentangling themselves from this, the officers urged the men into a double-quick, which, however, only encouraged the rioters, who looked upon it as a sign of fear and flight. New and increased crowds were soon met; they were threatened in rear and front, and a discharge of firearms began from sidewalks and windows. Then the order was given to return the fire. There was struggle, confusion, smoke, hooting, yells of "nigger thieves," "traitors," men dropping on the sidewalk and falling from windows, and wounded soldiers crawling feebly away under the feet of the rushing, howling mob.

Into the midst of this terror there suddenly came a little ray of hope and help. People began to shout, "Here comes the Mayor!" The city authorities, who had been waiting at the Washington Depot, had heard of the riot and were hastening to the rescue. The crowd fell back; a man came up, shook hands with Captain Follansbee, saying, "I am the Mayor of Baltimore." Mayor Brown courageously placed himself beside the captain, and, by voice and gesture, endeavored to quell the tumult, but to little purpose. The struggling, fighting column pushed ahead doggedly a square or two farther, the attack increasing rather than diminishing. The Mayor's own patience and temper was exhausted, and, seizing a gun from the hands of a soldier, he fired at and brought down one of the rioters.

At this point, Captain Follansbee states, the Mayor disappeared—most probably, as it would seem, because of the fortunate arrival of more effective help. Marshal Kane, chief of police, also hastening to the relief, here arrived on the scene of conflict with a squad of fifty policemen. Taking advantage of a favorable instant, he deployed his men in a line across the street, opened their ranks to allow the troops to pass through, and then, closing his line again, confronted the advancing mob with drawn revolvers. The movement diverted a moment's attention and checked the onward rush; the barrier held firm, the column of soldiers passed quickly on, and, though it met one or two slight additional attacks, it made its way to the Washington Depot. Here also there was a great crowd and excited tumult; the men were got into cars, and the train put into motion toward Washington under much difficulty; but no bloodshed occurred till at the last moment, when a shower of stones or a pistol-shot provoked a return volley from a window of the rear car, killing a prominent citizen. The number of casualties was never correctly ascertained. The soldiers lost four killed and some thirty wounded; the citizens probably two or three times as many.

With the departure of the Massachusetts Sixth, the Chief of Police supposed his immediate troubles at an end. But not yet; he was again notified that a new riot was beginning at the Philadelphia Depot. Hurrying there, he found that the regimental band had been left behind; and worse still, that a large number of cars constituting the rear end of the train, yet contained Small's Pennsylvania Brigade, numbering some thousand men, all unarmed. The former had already been driven from their car and scattered; the latter were just beginning to debark, entirely ignorant of what had happened. Gathering such of his policemen as were in the neighborhood, Marshal Kane intervened actively and with success for their temporary protection; and a hasty conference having been held with the railroad officers, the train was, by common consent, backed out of the depot and speedily despatched on its return toward Philadelphia.

These events took place in the forenoon, between ten and twelve o'clock. As the intelligence of the riot and its bloodshed was diffused through the great city, it called into immediate action the worst passions of the populace. For the remainder of the day the city was virtually at the mercy of the mob. By good fortune no general or widespread damage or spoliation occurred; but many minor acts of injury and law-breaking were perpetrated with impunity. Persons were maltreated, newspapers were mobbed, and stores and gunshops were broken into and robbed of their contents.

The secession conspirators were prompt in their endeavor to turn the incident to their own advantage. Under their management a mass meeting was called to meet that afternoon at four o'clock, in Monument Square, where, at the appointed hour, an immense concourse assembled. All the sweeping tide of popular sentiment ran against the Union and the North. There was not a National flag to be seen. The State flag of Maryland was displayed above the rostrum. In substance, most of the speeches were secession harangues. Denunciation of the soldiers, eulogies of the South, appeal and protest against invasion and coercion, met stormy applause. Governor Hicks was called to the stand, and yielding to the torrent of treasonable fury, made a short address which chimed in with the current outburst of hostile feeling. He intimated that the Union was broken, and that he was ready to bow before the will of the people. He would rather lose his right arm than raise it to strike a sister State.

Finding the Governor thus giving way, and the populace of Baltimore rising in response to their revolutionary promptings, the conspirators pushed forward their scheme of insurrection with all diligence, and succeeded in placing Maryland in a state of thorough revolt against the General Government, which lasted nearly a week. They prevailed on the Governor to call out the militia, which, under officers mostly inclined to secession, put all military acts and authority directly against the Union. They induced him to call a special session of the Legislature, and under the revolutionary terror of the hour, at a special election held in Baltimore the following week, a farcical minority vote was made to result in the choice of a city delegation to the Lower House, from among the rankest disunionists. They controlled the City Council, which, under plea of public defence, appropriated half a million to purchase and manufacture arms and gather the material of war. From Baltimore the furor spread to the country towns, where companies were raised and patrols established under the instructions and command of the secession militia general of Baltimore. Within a few days the United States flag practically disappeared from Maryland.

Their most effective act remains yet to be noticed. Near midnight of the day of the riot (April 19, 1861), the Mayor and police authorities made an official order (secret at the time, but subsequently avowed) to burn the nearest bridges on the railroads leading into Baltimore from the Free States, and immediately sent out different parties (the Chief of Police himself leading one of them), to execute the order.

Before daylight next morning, the bridges at Melvale, Relay House, and Cockeysville, on the Harrisburg road, and over the Bush and Gunpowder Rivers and Harris Creek on the Philadelphia road, were accordingly destroyed by fire, completely severing railroad communication with the North. The excuse was that they feared reprisal and revenge from the Northern armies ; the real motive appears to have been the stronger underlying spirit of insurrection.   Mayor Brown claimed that Governor Hicks approved the order ; the Governor soon afterward publicly and officially denied it. Whether Mayor Brown was a secession conspirator seems doubtful; but it is hard to resist the inference that the revolutionists influenced his action.   The controlling animus of the deed is clearly enough revealed in a telegram sent out that night by Marshal Kane :

" Thank you for your offer; bring your men in by the first train and we will arrange with the railroad afterward. Streets red with Maryland blood.   Send expresses over the mountains and valleys of Maryland and Virginia for the riflemen to come without delay.   Fresh hordes will be down on us to-morrow (the 20th).   We will fight them and whip them, or die."   This language at night, from the man who that morning had risked his life to protect the Massachusetts soldiers, sufficiently shows the overmastering outbreak of revolutionary madness.

CHAPTER VIII.

WASHINGTON.

In celebrating the attack and the fall of Sumter at Montgomery by a congratulatory speech and an official salute, the rebel Secretary of War ventured to predict that the Confederate flag would float over the capitol at Washington before the first of May. Whether this was to be accomplished by plot, by open military campaign, or through mere insurrectionary reversion, he did not explain. The idea, however, by long nursing and repeating, had become one of the fixed hopes of the rebellion. When the news of the Baltimore riot reached the South, the fulfilment of the prophecy was believed to be at hand. The revolt, which for a few days continually grew until it spread over all Maryland, served to deepen the universal impression. The Baltimore conspirators themselves were animated to fresh daring by their flattering local prospects. They sent at once to Richmond for a supply of arms. Governor Letcher responded with alacrity to their request. Senator Mason hastened to Baltimore to give them encouragement and advice. Two thousand muskets were forwarded with all possible despatch for their use. Twenty heavy guns were also ordered to be sent them a few days later, though it does not appear that the order could be fully executed. Meanwhile the Virginia rebels had possessed themselves of

Harper's Ferry and established a camp there, and from this vantage-ground they arranged a system of confidential communication with Baltimore. Nor was Richmond alone hopeful. Even Montgomery became inspired by the apparently favorable opportunity. Jefferson Davis telegraphed (April 22d) to Governor Letcher: "Sustain Baltimore, if practicable. We reinforce you," and ordered thirteen regiments to be concentrated in the "foreign country" of Virginia; and with all the confidence of a positive secret understanding, the rebel Secretary of War issued his requisitions upon the non-seceded Border Slave States to furnish a portion of this force.

In the North the bloody act of Baltimore raised the already seething war excitement to a pitch bordering on frenzy, and the public expressions of indignant wrath were in many instances disfigured by intemperate clamor for sweeping and indiscriminate vengeance upon that city. These ebullitions of hot blood were, however, everywhere wisely turned into increased ardor and effort to forward speedy relief and ample reinforcement to the Federal capital. The monster meeting of New York was held on the following day, at which a Union Defence Committee was formed from the foremost citizens of the great metropolis; and by this committee, money, ships, supplies, and marching regiments were provided and prepared to meet the threatening requirements of the hour.

Troops were, however, already on the way. Brigadier-General Butler, with the Eighth Massachusetts Regiment, reached Philadelphia on the afternoon of the riot. The famous Seventh Regiment of New York, under Colonel Lefferts, also arrived there on the following morning. Here the railroad officials gave the two commanders certain information of the burning of the railroad bridges and the im-

possibility of reaching Washington, or even Baltimore, by
the ordinary route, advising them, as an alternative, to proceed by water to Annapolis, and thence march overland to

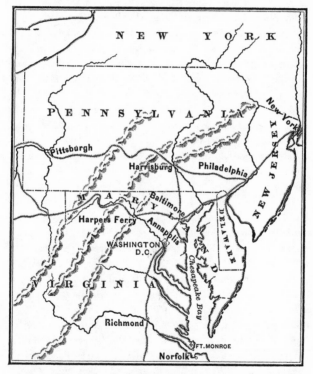

Routes of Approach to Washington

the capital. Acting as yet under separate State authority,
and unable to agree, the two regiments proceeded there by
different routes, one descending and the other ascending
Chesapeake Bay, Butler arriving in Annapolis harbor before

daylight, on Sunday morning, April 21st, and Lefferts joining him there next morning, Monday, April 22d.

On communicating with the shore, they were met by a
protest from Governor Hicks, warning them not to land.
With all his stubborn and ingrained loyalty, the Governor
was of a timid and somewhat vacillating nature, and for the
moment the clamor of the Baltimore mob overawed his
cooler judgment.   In this conflict between lawful duty and
popular pressure, he, too, caught at the flimsy plea of "State"
supremacy, and, in addition to presuming to forbid the
national flag on Maryland soil, wrote a letter to the President, asking that the troops be ordered elsewhere, and
suggesting that Lord Lyons, the British Minister, be requested to mediate between the Government and the rebels,
a proposal which was at once answered by a dignified rebuke
from Mr. Seward.

The administration at Washington had not been unmind-
ful of the dangerous condition of Maryland; but great reliance was placed upon the discretion and loyalty of Governor
Hicks to avert danger.   He had held several personal consultations with the President and Secretary of War; had
agreed to hold his people in check, and furnish four Maryland regiments of picked Union men under the call; and to
make his compliance easier, the authorities consented that
these should not be ordered South, but kept on service in
their own State, or in the District of Columbia.   The Governor was frank enough to acknowledge his failure to keep his
engagement.   "We were arranging and organizing forces,"
he wrote, "to protect the city and preserve order, but want
of organization, of arms, prevented success.   They had arms,
they had the principal part of the organized military forces
with them; and for us to have made the effort under the circumstances, would have had the effect to aid the disorderly

element. They took possession of the armories, have the arms and ammunition, and I therefore think it prudent to decline (for the present) responding affirmatively to the requisition made by President Lincoln for four regiments of infantry."

Unfortunately the disaster at Baltimore did not come single-handed. At the picturesque little town of Harper's Ferry, where the Potomac River flows through one of the gateways in the Blue Ridge, the United States had an extensive armory, containing much valuable machinery for the manufacture of rifles and muskets, originally located there because of the convenient and cheap water-power which the river affords. The town was famous as the scene of John Brown's invasion and capture. The seizure of this place with its works and its supposed strategical importance was an essential item in the conspiracy. A small company of regulars had been guarding it since January. One of General Scott's first orders was to have a volunteer regiment detached to reinforce it, a precaution which could not be taken earlier because of the want of troops. With the quick secession of Virginia, however, the proposed help came too late. Governor Letcher pushed forward his State forces to menace the place with such haste, that, on the night of April 18th, Lieutenant Jones set fire to the establishment and withdrew his sixty men through Maryland into Pennsylvania. The Rebels immediately took possession, and though the fire had done much damage, the principal part of the machinery was rescued by them and afterward sent to Richmond. As already mentioned, a rebel camp was immediately established, and its force in a few days augmented to two thousand four hundred men—doubtless with a view to join rebellious Maryland in a descent upon Washington.

Serious as was the loss of Harper's Ferry, a sacrifice of infinitely greater proportions almost immediately followed.

Near Norfolk, Va., was one of the principal naval stations of the Government, the Gosport Navy Yard. This, too, was one of the prizes coveted by the conspirators ; its buildings, supplies, machinery, dry dock, and especially a number of valuable ships, constituted a money value amounting to many millions ; and the importance of their possession and use to either the insurgents or the Government, in a rebellion, was of course immeasurable. Beyond mere occupancy by a few officers and a little handful of marines, the place was without substantial protection. The Lincoln administration had fully realized its exposure, but for want of troops could send it no early reinforcements. Such measures of precaution as were possible had long since been taken. The officers had been admonished to vigilance, and preparation made to bring away the more valuable ships. It was General Scott's design to advance troops to its support the moment Fortress Monroe should be secure.

Under these circumstances occurred the sudden fall of Sumter, the President's proclamation, the secession of Virginia, and the immediate movement of Governor Letcher's State forces against both Harper's Ferry and Gosport. As a preliminary act, he thought to absolutely prevent the escape of the ships by obstructing Elizabeth River with small sunken vessels. The device did not completely succeed, though it greatly enhanced the danger. It is possible that all might yet have been ultimately saved, but for a contingency against which foresight was impossible. The ships were ready to move out ; the most valuable of them—the Merrimack—had steam up and was on point of sailing, when, by the treachery and false counsel of his subordinate officers, Commandant McCauley, of the navy yard, whose loyalty had hitherto not been suspected, revoked his permission to let her depart.

The officers charged with the removal hurried to Washington to obtain superior orders; but their absence and the necessary delay only rendered the situation worse. When they returned with a ship-of-war and a regiment, they found that, through a repetition of treasonable advice, the ships had been scuttled and were sinking. It was decided that neither rescue nor defence was now possible; and on the night of April 20th, the officers of the relieving expedition undertook to destroy the yard, property, and all the ships, except one, in a great conflagration, to prevent their falling into rebel hands—an attempt, however, which proved only partially successful. Whether or not the actual emergency justified this enormous sacrifice, will perhaps always remain an open question among military experts. It was as necessary for the Administration to confide to the officers this discretion, as similar discretion in any military enterprise. They seem to have acted in good faith and upon their best judgment, and their action was accepted, perhaps with regret, but with full acquittal of duty conscientiously discharged.

It may well be imagined that the authorities and inhabitants of the national capital watched the development of rebellion in the neighboring States of Virginia and Maryland with the keenest anxiety. Washington, in tradition, tone, and aspiration, was essentially a Southern city. Slavery existed and the local slave-trade flourished here; in latter times the maintenance of the institution in the District of Columbia formed a distinct plank in Democratic platforms. Southern arrogance and Southern ambition had long dominated official society. All the cant and all the sneers of the *haut ton* of the capital were vented against mercenary Yankeedom, and the rustic and provincial West, which had won the late presidential election. The confusion and controversy of faction exhibited during the winter session of Con-

gress shook the faith of many a political veteran. The secession harangues of conspicuous fire-eaters were openly ap-
plauded from the House and Senate galleries. As the social
lights faded one by one from the Congressional corridors
and the promenades of Lafayette Park and Pennsylvania
Avenue, the social sympathies of Washington to a large extent followed them into the eclipse of their "foreign" confederacy. These too, notwithstanding their complaints and
defiance, departed with an evident reluctance and regret
into a country without a capital, and whose social and official circles were yet in embryo. A few were so unguarded
as to distribute confidential nods and winks that they expected soon to return; while no doubt all nursed the long-
ing hope that at no distant day they might reclaim and re-
enter the city as their proper and natural heritage. It was
this almost universal Southern feeling which found expression in the prediction of the rebel Secretary of War, that the
rebel flag would float over the dome of the capitol before
the first of May.

There was, therefore, great doubt about the disposition
and loyalty of the resident population; and the startling
succession of disasters to the Union cause created a pro-
found impression. Virginia's secession on the 17th; Harper's Ferry lost on the 18th; Baltimore in arms, and the
North effectually cut off on the 19th; the Gosport Navy
Yard sacrificed on the 20th—where would the tide of misfortune stop? Wavering Unionists found no great difficulty
in forecasting the final success of rebellion; sanguine secessionists already in their visions saw the stars and stripes
banished to the north of Mason and Dixon's line.

Whatever the doubt, there was no other present resource
but to rely largely upon the good faith and order of Washington City. The whole matter had been under the almost

constant investigation of General Scott and his subordinates since January; and officers of earnestness and good judgment assured him that the local militia would stand by the Government and the flag. In that assurance fifteen companies of volunteers had, since the 9th of April, been enlisted, equipped, and armed for the defence of the city. A few individuals out of these companies refused, at the last moment, to take the oath of enlistment, and were publicly disgraced; but the remainder went into the service cheerfully, and, so far as is known, served their term loyally and honorably.

Chiefly, however, General Scott relied on some six companies of troops from the regular army, which he had concentrated from various parts of the country in scattering driblets, among them being two light batteries of exceptionally good discipline and drill. These, together with a small force of marines to guard the marine barracks, were stationed at the critical points in the city; secret instructions were issued to designated officers to hurry, in case of alarm, to the charge and command of various public buildings specially prepared to resist sudden ingress or capture, and stored with ammunition and provisions against temporary siege; and pickets and patrols were sent out to watch all the leading roads and bridges.

To aid these, there had arrived in the city two detachments of volunteers from other States; the first, some three or four hundred Pennsylvanians, on the evening of April 18th, who were armed and equipped after their arrival; the second, the compact and courageous Massachusetts Sixth Regiment, on the evening of April 19th, after having, as already detailed, fought its way through Baltimore. This regiment was at once quartered in the Senate Chamber at the Capitol, which, with its extemporized barricades, began to take on the frowning aspect of a fort.

From the officers and men of this regiment the President and other authorities learned verbally the dangerous character and proportions of the Baltimore riot. This occurred on Friday. Saturday brought him not only many letters and telegrams setting forth the details and increasing signs of disaffection, but a committee from the Baltimore authorities, to verbally represent the unrestrained turbulence of the city, and to urge that further bloodshed be avoided by stopping the transit of troops. General Scott, to whom the request was at once referred, desiring the speedy presence of volunteers to defend Washington rather than to fight a battle in Baltimore, suggested that they might be marched around, instead of being brought through, that city. To this suggestion President Lincoln readily agreed, and the committee assented to the arrangement. On the following day, Sunday, however, local riot had risen to general insurrection in Maryland, and the authorities of Baltimore, called to Washington by the President, now put forth the request that no more troops be brought through Maryland. This demand the President and Cabinet summarily rejected. It was agreed, however, that, if no resistance were offered to their march, either around Baltimore or by way of Annapolis, they would not be forced through the city, and with that assurance the committee departed.

Pending this discussion rumors came that a portion of the Pennsylvania forces were advancing on Baltimore by way of the route from Harrisburg, and the committee soon returned, reporting a fresh turmoil in Baltimore, and an arming *en masse* to resist their passage. The movement was unknown to the President; and to disabuse the Baltimoreans of any possible imputation of bad faith, Lincoln ordered that the detachment complained of should return to Harrisburg, and come round by way of Annapolis; also, however, giving the committee formal notice that he would not thereafter again interfere to change mere military details. This order was, at the time, the occasion of much outcry against the President from excited critics who totally misapprehended its scope and spirit. It simply changed a dangerous, perhaps impossible march, to one practicable and comparatively secure; it did not surrender a general right, but only yielded a non-essential point to gain a real military advantage for Washington.

The burning of the railroad bridges east and north of Baltimore had permanently interrupted communication before daylight, on the morning of Saturday, April 20th; on Sunday night, April 21st, the insurrectionary authorities in the same place took possession of the telegraph offices and wires, and Washington went into the condition of an isolated and blockaded city. Both from the Virginia and the Maryland side there came exaggerated rumors of gathering hostile forces, and preparations for a *coup de main* against the capital; and, though not actually or visibly threatened, the city was in the very nature of things forced into the privations and inconveniences of a siege. Military arrangements and military regulations became everywhere the rule. The public buildings were hedged with barricades and guarded by sentinels. The little steamers on the Potomac, and the stores of flour and grain in the Georgetown mills were seized by the Government. Squads of cavalry dashed through the streets. Business practically ceased; the life and bustle of the city was hushed. Mere sojourners, and even many residents, took alarm, and hurried away by private conveyance. The hotels, which had a week before been thronged to overflowing, became deserted, or were haunted by only a few mute and white-faced guests, who looked like apparitions in contrast with their recent gayety.

As the gloom increased there began to be talk of general military impressment for the defence of the city. This had the effect of finally exposing the loyalty or disloyalty of many Washington officers, clerks, residents, and *habitués* who had maintained a dubious silence. On Monday, April 22d, quite a stampede took place into Virginia and the South; some hundreds of clerks from the various departments of Government, and a considerable number of officers of the army and navy, hitherto unable to decide between their treasonable inclinations and the attractions of their salaries, finally resigned, and cast their fortunes with the Rebellion.

The routine work of the departments went on with its machine-like monotony; the cabinet members called on the President and discussed chances and rumors; General Scott conferred with his subordinates, and made daily confidential reports to Lincoln. The situation, however, revealed nothing certain or definite. From the windows of the Executive Mansion a rebel flag could be seen flying at Alexandria. One rumor asserted that a hostile detachment was being assembled near Mount Vernon; a second, that an attack on Fort Washington was imminent; a third, that an investing force was being brought down from Harper's Ferry. *Per contra*, there came the welcome information that there were ships and volunteers at Annapolis; but it was clouded with the rumor that their landing would be disputed and their march obstructed by Baltimore roughs and Maryland militia. A pioneer train reported the railroad safe to the Junction, but nothing could be learned of its condition beyond; while several messengers, despatched to reach Annapolis, had returned unsuccessful. What was transpiring in the outer world could only be surmised; whether danger lurked far or near was a mystery incapable of present solution. Nevertheless, the President and Cabinet were not only calm, but hopeful, under General Scott's assurance that, with his present force, the city and all the public buildings were entirely safe against ten thousand troops not better than the District volunteers.

In point of fact, after some diplomacy with the Governor and Mayor, the Massachusetts Eighth and New York Seventh had really landed at Annapolis on Monday afternoon, April 22d; and, after still further delay in sifting threatening rumors, in a somewhat deliberate local reconnoissance, and in repairing a disabled locomotive, the two regiments started on their march toward Washington, on Wednesday, the 24th. A year or two later this would have been considered tardy movement under the requirements of urgent danger; but, considering the surprise, the anxiety, the suspicions and uncertainties, and the want of preparation amid which they acted, there is much to excuse their caution and delay. They had few rations and no transportation. Full of high, patriotic zeal, they were new to the trials and privations of an actual campaign, even of so mild a type. Once started, however, they pushed ahead with pluck and perseverance, and by daylight next morning reached Annapolis Junction— a distance of some twenty miles—without opposition, having repaired the railroad track as they advanced. At the Junction they found a railroad train in waiting, which, two hours later, landed the famous "Seventh" at the capital. Then came their hour of peaceful triumph, in which they forgot their hunger and thirst, their bridge-building in the broiling sun, and their foot-sore scouting through .the tedious midnight hours. Debarking from the cars amid the welcome-shouts of an assembled throng, and forming with all the ready precision of their holiday drill, they marched with exultant music and gayly fluttering banners up Pennsylvania

Avenue to the Executive Mansion, to receive the President's thankful salute.   With their arrival, about noon of the 25th of April, all the gloom, and doubt, and feeling of danger to the capital, vanished.   In comparison with the unmurmuring endurance that trudged through the Yazoo swamps, and the unflinching courage that faced the dreadful carnage of the Wilderness, later in the war, this march of the "Seventh" was the merest regimental picnic; but it has become historic because it marked a turning-point in the national destiny, and signified the will of the people that the capital of the Union should remain where George Washington planted it.

CHAPTER IX.

It has already been related in a previous chapter how the incidents immediately following the fall of Sumter and the President's Proclamation—the secession of Virginia and the adhesion of other Border States—had doubled the strength and augmented the war preparations of the Rebellion. Upon the Government and the people of the North the experience of those eventful days was even more decisive. Whatever hope President Lincoln and his Cabinet may have entertained at the beginning, that secession could be controlled by the suppression of sporadic insurrections and the reawakening of the slumbering or intimidated loyalty of the South, necessarily faded out before the loss of Virginia, North Carolina, Tennessee, and Arkansas, and the dangerous uprising in Maryland. Not alone prompt measures to save the capital of the nation were imperatively dictated by the sudden blockade and isolation of Washington, but widespread civil war, waged by a gigantic army and navy, must become the inevitable price of maintaining the Union. For this work the seventy-five thousand three-months militia were clearly inadequate. It marks President Lincoln's accurate diagnosis of the public danger, and his prompt courage and action to avert it, that, as early as April 26th, ten days after the first proclamation, the formation of a new army had already been resolved upon; and the War Department began giving official notice that volunteers in excess of the first call could only be received for three years or during the war, the details of the new organizations, to consist of 42,034 volunteers, 22,714 regulars, and 18,000 seamen, being publicly announced on May 3d. No express provision of law existed for these measures, but Lincoln ordered them without hesitation, because the exigency did not admit of even the short delay of awaiting the assemblage of Congress. He was too true a type and representative of the people to doubt one instant their sure support and approval of a step which the Constitution covered with its paramount authority, and its imperative personal mandate to the President of the United States to "preserve, protect, and defend the Constitution of the United States."

Following the march of the Seventh Regiment, the Annapolis route remained permanently open to the Union troops from the North. Day by day vessels arrived in Annapolis Harbor with volunteer regiments, with provisions and supplies for their maintenance, with war material for their equipment. These were transferred rapidly over the repaired railroad to Washington City, and it was not long before the National Capital resembled a great military camp. Troops found temporary lodgment in the various public buildings; citizen recruits wrote letters home on the senators' desks, spouted buncombe for pastime from the members' seats in the House of Representatives, spread their blankets for bivouac in the ample corridors of the Patent Office; clusters of tents filled the public squares; regimental tactics, practice in platoon-firing and artillery-drill went on in the surrounding fields; inspection and dress parade became fashionable entertainments; military bands furnished unceasing open-air concerts; the city bloomed with national flags. The presence of an army brought an influx of civilians that at once perceptibly augmented the floating population; and this Yankee invasion of a sleepy Southern city gave Washington a baptism of Northern life, activity, business, trade, and enterprise, which, for the first time after half a century of sickly pining, made the metropolitan dreams of its founder a substantial hope and possibility.

Under the vast enlargement of military operations to which the defence and maintenance of the Government was now driven by inexorable events, the utility and employment of the three-months volunteers became necessarily limited and confined to a few local objects. The mature experience and judgment of General Scott decided that it would be useless, considering their very short term of service, to undertake with their help more than the garrisoning of Fort Monroe, the protection of the Potomac, the defence of Washington City, the restoration of the military routes through Baltimore to the North and West, the political control of Maryland, and possibly the recapture of Harper's Ferry—a programme forming practically one combined measure—the defence of the military frontier or line of the Potomac, from the sea to the mountains. Larger projects must be postponed for preparation; ships must be improvised or built to enforce the blockade; a new army must be gathered to open the Mississippi and restore authority in the South.

The rebels, though now seriously checked, were yet industriously working their local conspiracy in Maryland to secure the final complete insurrection and adhesion of that State. The Legislature, apparently under their control, had met at Frederick, and was devising legislation under which to set up a military dictatorship. But the Administration at Washington allowed them no time to gather strength at home, or draw any considerable supplies or help from Virginia. The

President authorized General Scott to suspend the privilege
of the writ of *habeas corpus* within certain limits, and empowered him to arrest or disperse the Legislature in case
they attempted treason.   Annapolis was garrisoned and
lightly fortified ; a military guard was pushed along the railroads toward Baltimore simultaneously from the South and
the North ; and, on May 13th, General Butler, by a bold,
though entirely unauthorized movement, entered the city in
the dusk of evening, while a convenient thunder-storm was
raging, with less than a thousand men, part of whom were
the now famous Massachusetts Sixth, and during the night
entrenched himself on Federal Hill.   General Scott repri-
manded the "hazardous" movement ; nevertheless, the little
garrison met no further molestation or attack, and soon,
supported by other detachments, open resistance to the
Government disappeared from the entire State.   Independent regiments of Maryland volunteers entered the Federal
service ; a sweeping political reaction also set in, demonstrat-
ing that the Union sentiment was largely predominant ; between which and the presence of Union troops the legislative intrigue was blighted, and the persistent secession
minority and almost irrepressible local conspiracy were effectually baffled, though not without constant vigilance and
severe discipline throughout the remainder of the year.

While the Government was thus mainly occupied in restoring its authority in Maryland, the rebels were busy in
military organization in various parts of Virginia.   Among
the resignations from the Federal army were two officers of
especial prominence—Joseph E. Johnston, Quartermaster-
General, of the rank of Brigadier-General, and Robert E.
Lee, lately promoted to be Colonel of the First Cavalry.
Lee was an officer of great promise, and a personal favorite
of General Scott, who at once conceived the idea of putting

him at the head of the Union army about to take the field; and, on Saturday, April 20th, an informal and unofficial tender of this honor appears to have been made to him by Francis P. Blair, senior, as coming from President Lincoln. In a letter written subsequent to the war, Lee says that he declined this offer. That same evening he wrote a resignation from Arlington, and on Monday hurried off to Richmond, where he was appointed by Governor Letcher, and, on April 23d, publicly installed to command the military forces of Virginia.

Lee did not share the radical clamor of many of the Richmond conspirators for an immediate advance to capture Washington. He discouraged mere reckless enthusiasm, and urged a defensive policy and methodical and thorough military preparation. Carrying out this policy in his orders, directions were issued, and officers sent to different localities to call out and organize the State militia, to drill recruits, and collect materials and stores. Under his management companies and regiments soon sprang up, and Virginia, like the other Southern States, gradually became a general camp. It was not a great while before the presence of a military force at the principal points along the Potomac became evident. Its concentration and offensive action either to close the river to navigation, or, when sufficiently strong, against Washington, was, of course, only a question of time. The contact of hostile armies unavoidably provokes conflict.

These changing conditions of Virginia required new precautions for the defence of Washington. As early as May 3d it was ascertained by the local officers and engineers that the Capitol building was only three and a half miles from Arlington Heights on the Virginia side of the river, the Executive Mansion and various department buildings but two and a half, and Georgetown within one mile. The enemy already had a detachment quartered at Alexandria; re-inforcements from the South might, in a single night, occupy the heights and destroy the Virginia end of the bridges, and, speedily erecting mortar batteries, could destroy the city with bombs, unless they were attacked at a disadvantage and dislodged. It was, therefore, decided that the Union forces must occupy Arlington Heights to insure the safety of the city, though the necessary troops could not as yet be spared from the operations to secure Maryland; and by reason of various delays, three weeks more passed away before the full preparations for the enterprise were completed.

Finally, at two o'clock on the morning of May 24th, three columns crossed the Potomac and entered on the "sacred soil" of the Old Dominion: three regiments by the Aqueduct at Georgetown, four regiments by the Long Bridge from Washington, and one regiment, Ellsworth's Zouaves, from their camp below the city directly by steamer to Alexandria, the war steamer Pawnee being anchored off shore to protect the landing. The movement met no opposition; no considerable rebel force was stationed at the bridges, and the detachment at Alexandria, excepting a small troop of cavalry, which was captured, evacuated that place on receiving a notice, sent without authority by the commander of the Pawnee, to surrender or retire.

It had been a beautiful moonlight night; all the regiments were filled with an eager enthusiasm for the march; the preparations were careful, the officers to supervise it intelligent and competent, the movements promptly begun and successfully completed. The whole enterprise seemed on the very point of conclusion without an accident, when sudden news of the assassination of Colonel Ellsworth not only saddened the camps on both sides of the Potomac, but cast a new gloom, and spread a feeling of bitter vindictiveness throughout every loyal State.

Colonel Ellsworth was a young man of twenty-four, who, by the possession of a phenomenal combination of genius, energy, and self-confidence, had won the attention and admiration of the whole country. But a few years ago, foiled by misfortune in an attempt to begin professional life in Chicago, he had suddenly found himself without money or friends—almost without bread. By the endurance of extreme privations, the pittance which he managed to earn with some temporary writing kept off starvation. His energetic nature made active occupation a necessity; and perhaps as much to consume the evening hours, as with any other fixed purpose, he became interested in studying and teaching others the manual of military drill. This led to the formation of a little volunteer company of about sixty Chicago youths—clerks and business employees—under his command. Into their instruction he threw such a degree of enthusiasm, such originality in remodelling and adapting old methods, such a grasp of purpose, and such a genius of control, that, after about a year's training, he not only carried off the prizes for drill at the fairs and exhibitions in the neighboring counties, but confidently formed the bold project of showing to the public of the great cities that he had the best-drilled company in America.

They had no money, no commissariat, no transportation, but a friendly railroad gave them free tickets from Chicago to Detroit; from there the proceeds of an exhibition drill carried them to the next city, and so on. At every step of their progress, their actual dexterity in the manual of arms carried admiration and applause by storm. Arrived at New York, they achieved a double triumph; first before the uniformed city militia in the open field, and afterward at night

on the stage of the Academy of Music, before as fashionable
an audience as ever packed the walls or split their kid gloves
to encore the most famous prima donna.   For three days the
metropolitan newspapers were full of descriptions of their
performance and their personal appearance and history—
above all, of their youthful commander, Ellsworth, the visible
creator, embodiment, and inspiration of their admirable
accomplishment.   Determined to leave no test unchallenged,
they went even to show their proficiency to the military
school at West Point, where the only criticism that could be
passed upon them was that they did not follow the "regular" drill of the text-books.   When they finally returned to
Chicago, after a full tour, in which they had reaped uninterrupted encouragement and acclaim, the name and fame of
Ellsworth and his "Chicago Zouaves" were a part of the
just interest and pride of the whole country.

Nevertheless, no one appreciated better than Ellsworth
himself that this was but a possible beginning of better
things.   He had no ambition to remain either a mere drill-
master or a raree showman, though his necessities had compelled him to make a somewhat spectacular beginning.
There is not room here to trace his higher purposes and
ideals of a general militia reform; it is sufficient to say that
for the brain of a boy of twenty-four they were serious and
comprehensive.   There was then no thought of war; and
when Lincoln became President, Ellsworth sought his favor
and was readily permitted to accompany him to Washington
as one of his suite.   The inauguration over, the President
made him a second lieutenant of dragoons.   Then came
Sumter and the call for volunteers, and Ellsworth saw his
opportunity.   Hastening to the city of New York, he called
together and harangued the fire companies of the metropolis; in three days he had twenty-two hundred names in-

scribed on his recruiting lists; out of these he carefully selected a regiment of eleven hundred men, who chose him their colonel, and, bearing half a dozen beautiful presentation flags, one of them publicly donated by Mrs. Astor, followed him to Washington, where they were mustered into the service among the earliest three years volunteers.

It was at the head of this regiment that Colonel Ellsworth entered Alexandria at daylight of May 24th. The rebels received notice of his coming, and most of them retired with sufficient promptness to escape capture. Having seen the town securely occupied and pickets posted to prevent surprise, Colonel Ellsworth remembered the rebel flag which had been for weeks flaunting an insulting defiance to the national capital. It was hoisted over the Marshall House, the principal hotel of Alexandria, and the Colonel was seized with the whim to take it down with his own hands—a foolish fancy, perhaps, when considered in cool judgment, but one very natural to the heated enthusiasm of those early days of burning patriotic ardor. "Whose flag is that flying over this house?" demanded he, as he entered and ascended the stairs. "I don't know," was the only response he could obtain; but the demon of a hellish purpose lurked under the answer. He mounted to the roof with one or two companions, cut the halyards, and started down with the treasonable emblem on his arm. The stairs were narrow and winding— they could descend only in single file—a soldier preceded and followed him. As he reached the third step above the landing on the second floor, a side door flew open, and the owner of the house, a man named Jackson, who had been lurking there in concealment like a tiger for his prey, sprang out, and levelling a double-barrelled shotgun, discharged it full in the Colonel's breast—the fatal charge driving almost into his very heart a gold presentation badge inscribed "Non

8

nobis sed pro patria." Ellsworth fell forward in death without even a groan; but the murder did not go unavenged, for in that same instant his assassin also expired by the double effect of a musket-charge and a bayonet-thrust from Ellsworth's foremost companion.

If there remained a possibility of a sensational climax of deeper import than Sumter and Baltimore, it was furnished by this hideous tragedy at Alexandria. The North had supposed that the first exhausted the cold-blooded recklessness of conspiracy. The second manifested the sudden fury of sectional excitement. But this last opened an unlooked-for depth of individual hatred, into which the political animosities of years between the North and South had finally ripened after four months of uninterrupted manipulation by the conspiracy. Under this unwelcome revelation there was no longer room to doubt the existence of widely pervading elements of an enduring civil war. Ellsworth was buried with imposing honors, from the famous East Room of the Executive Mansion, the President, Cabinet, and high officers of Government attending as mourners ; and as the telegraph filled the newspapers with details of the sad event, every household in the North felt as if the dark shadow of a funeral had lowered over its own hearthstone.

CHAPTER X.

MISSOURI.

CONSPIRACY had been working with untiring persistence in every Slave State since, and even before, the formal secession of the Cotton States in January, and had everywhere made considerable advances, notably in the State of Missouri. Governor Jackson, of that State, had leagued himself with the secession plot, though still concealing his purpose with outward professions of loyalty. Many subordinate officers and members of the Legislature were secretly aiding him. Together they were leading Missouri through the usual and well-established paths to ultimate treason, by means of official recommendations from the Governor and various shrewdly devised laws passed by the Legislature. They made a serious miscalculation, however, in the stereotyped and hitherto always successful expedient of a State Convention. When that body was elected and met (February 28th), it showed such an overwhelming majority of Union members, that the plotters of treason were quite willing to hide their defeat in joining certain pointed declarations by the convention against secession, and adjourning its sittings to the following December, trusting their chances to a more pliant and treasonable legislature; hoping to bring about a policy of arming the State under pretence of local defence, and committing it to a neutral attitude under plea of local security. In all their efforts, however, they met the constant and determined watchfulness and opposition of zealous and fearless Unionists, among whom Frank P. Blair, junior, was a conspicuous leader.

It so happened, also, that in this State a small detachment of the regular army was, for the first time, rendered useful in thwarting the local development of disunion. At the city of St. Louis was an arsenal belonging to the United States, containing a considerable quantity of arms and ammunition. To obtain these was from the beginning, as in other States, a prime object of Governor Jackson and his co-conspirators. They had in January, as they believed, perfected an intrigue for the surrender of the arsenal, by the officer in charge, into their hands and control. That arrangement was soon blighted by the arrival of reinforcements ordered there by General Scott to protect the place, under command of an officer afterward famous—Captain Nathaniel Lyon, of the Second United States Infantry.

Lyon was a man of outspoken anti-slavery principles, of unswerving loyalty to his flag, and of unsleeping vigilance over his post and the Government interests. By the middle of February enough recruits had been added by General Scott to his own company of eighty trained regulars to raise his force to four hundred and eighty-eight men.

Holding the same political convictions and patriotic impulses, Lyon and Blair became quickly united in an intimate personal friendship; and very soon, also, Lyon's regulars and Blair's "Home Guards" sustained each other in a mutual reliance and protection. Their common watchfulness over the arsenal was by no means wasted. Governor Jackson was determined to establish by force what he had failed to accomplish by intrigue. He sent two trusty agents to the Rebel President to solicit help in arms and ammunition. "After learning," wrote Jefferson Davis, in reply, April 23d, "as well as I could from the gentlemen accredited to me, what was most needful for the attack on the arsenal, I have directed that Captains Green and Duke should be furnished with two twelve-pounder howitzers and two thirty-two-pounder guns, with the proper ammunition for each. These, from the commanding hills, will be effective, both against the garrison, and to breach the enclosing walls of the place."

Encouraged by this co-operation, the Governor, as his next step, instructed one of his militia generals, D. M. Frost, a West Point graduate, to assemble the available organized and equipped volunteer companies of the State in a camp of instruction at St. Louis. The Governor had also convened his Rebel Legislature to meet in extra session on May 2d. The day following, May 3d, began the assembling of the militia in "Camp Jackson," so named in honor of the Governor. Two regiments and part of a third soon arrived; and though some of the companies were either without political bias, or of Union sentiment, a general spirit of secession pervaded the camp, and its avenues were christened "Davis" and "Beauregard." The object of the organization soon became unmistakably known to Lyon, Blair, and the Union Safety Committee, who, by the aid of skilful detectives, gained information of all its movements. On the night of May 8th, the cannon, ammunition, and some muskets furnished by Jefferson Davis, were landed from a New Orleans steamer, in boxes marked "marble," and immediately loaded upon drays and hauled out to the camp.

Under this threatening disclosure, the Unionists felt they could no longer dally with the conspiracy. Already three weeks before, the United States Arsenal at Liberty, Mo., had been robbed of its arms by the disunionists, and Jeff.

Thompson was known to be actively drilling rebel companies at St. Joseph. They could not afford to allow a concentration of these and other treasonable forces. In the meanwhile the Washington authorities, receiving Governor Jackson's insulting refusal to furnish troops, had ordered the enlistment of Blair's "Home Guards" into the United States service, to the number of four regiments, which order was soon increased to ten thousand men.

With this force Lyon felt himself strong enough to crush the budding insurrection. On the morning of May 9th he disguised himself in female garb, and, seating himself beside a friend in a barouche, was driven out into Camp Jackson, personally and leisurely inspecting its strength, situation, and military approaches. The next day the arsenal and the various volunteer armories were alive with military preparation, and, at two o'clock in the afternoon, Lyon, at the head of his battalion of regulars, with six pieces of artillery and six regiments from the lately organized Missouri Volunteers and Reserve Corps (as they were respectively called), marched rapidly through various streets of St. Louis, in two columns, concentrating at Camp Jackson. Before General Frost was well aware of the coming event, these regiments had surrounded his camp and posted the batteries on commanding elevations. The camp thus invested, with batteries and arms ready for instant action, Lyon sent Frost a note, stating that his command was regarded as hostile to the United States, and demanding an immediate surrender, "with no other conditions than that all persons surrendering under this demand shall be humanely and kindly treated," and allowing half an hour's time for compliance. The circumstances left Frost no alternative, and before the expiration of the half-hour he gave notice of his unconditional surrender.

So far everything had gone as harmlessly as if the affair were merely a gala parade ; but now a most deplorable occurrence succeeded. The march, the halt, and the capture greatly excited a vast crowd which the occasion drew together; and scarcely had the homeward march with the prisoners begun, when the troops were assailed by secession rowdies with abusive language, stones, missiles, and finally a pistol shot or two. This last provoked a return volley without orders from one or two companies, by which, and the desultory shots succeeding, fifteen to twenty innocent bystanders and several soldiers were instantly killed. The untoward incident caused a dangerous ferment in the city, but the courageous efforts of the police prevented a general riot.

The telegraphic news of the capture of Camp Jackson threw the Governor's revolutionary cabal and disloyal legislature sitting at Jefferson City into the utmost consternation. The Governor immediately sent out and caused a bridge on the railroad from St. Louis to be burned, to prevent any sudden descent by Lyon upon the capital ; and during the afternoon and night, the Legislature in secret session rushed through several acts specially designed to promote rebellion, which they had before been concocting with more circumspection. A few days later, a military bill, virtually making the Governor an irresponsible military dictator, was formally passed ; and having thus, as the conspirators thought, made all necessary legal preparations, the session was finally adjourned on May 15th.

General Harney, the ranking officer in the Department of the West, who had been temporarily called away, returned to St. Louis the day after the Camp Jackson affair, thus superseding Lyon in command. It must be explained that events, and particularly antecedent conditions, had most unfortu-

nately divided the Missouri Unionists into two bitterly an-
tagonistic factions, which, indeed, continued throughout the
whole four years' war. The Radicals, embracing the large
German population of St. Louis, and who formed the bulk
of the Home Guard, were mainly of democratic antecedents,
and strong anti-slavery sentiment; these followed the leadership of Blair and Lyon. The Conservatives, more generally
of American nativity, belonging rather to the wealthy and
the business classes of the city, largely of Whig antecedents
and strongly tinged with the "Know-Nothing" prejudices of
former years, and holding very tolerant if not actually
favorable sentiments toward slavery, grouped themselves
about General Harney. The Radicals believed in defending
the Government with steel and lead; the Conservatives
trusted to reclaim their erring brethren with forbearance and
moral suasion. Cold after-criticism finds both factions
chargeable with extremes of feeling and speech; but if the
former were prone to excessive zeal, the latter were yet more
culpable in a stupid over-caution. Such deep local antago-
nisms, however, of nationality, class, and life-long political
prejudice, can hardly be expected to act with moderation in
the blinding atmosphere of revolution.

Harney was a loyal and courageous soldier, but lacked the
quick, instinctive judgment of the statesman. Beset by noisy
clamor on both sides, he vibrated to acts of conflicting
rather than consistent administration. His first impulse was
to order the disbandment of the Home Guards. Convinced
that this was beyond his power, he soon after (May 14th)
issued his proclamation justifying the capture of Camp
Jackson, denouncing the Military Bill as an indirect secession ordinance, and declaring that "Missouri must share the
destiny of the Union." He also announced his determination to uphold the Government of the United States "at all

times and under all circumstances;" but his measures to carry out this loyal policy were not chosen with wisdom.

Governor Jackson had at once proceeded to organize the militia of Missouri under his dictatorial military bill; and Frost's military laurels having withered at Camp Jackson, the Governor made ex-Governor Sterling Price his general-in-chief. Price was less scrupulous in political strategy than Harney, and within a week he had entrapped the unwary Union commander into an agreement which tied up the Government forces in a rôle of mere idle lookers-on, while Governor Jackson's Missouri militia should without hinderance place the State in active insurrection.

"General Price," so ran the agreement, signed on May 21st, "having by commission full authority over the militia of the State of Missouri, undertakes, with the sanction of the Governor of the State, already declared, to direct the whole power of the State officers to maintain order within the State among the people thereof; and General Harney publicly declares that, this object being thus assured, he can have no occasion, as he has no wish, to make military movements which might otherwise create excitements and jealousies, which he most earnestly desires to avoid."

This was to be done "in subordination to the laws of the General and State Governments;" but it gave the conspirators the right of initiative, and left them for a season the uncontrolled, and even unobserved masters of the whole State outside of St. Louis. Governor Jackson and General Price made such prompt use of their time, that before the end of the month reports of outrageous indignities upon Union men came from all parts of the State, and finally the threatening rumor that a rebel invasion from the Arkansas border was being encouraged and rapidly formed; and as fast as Harney brought the facts to the notice of Price, that dissembling conspirator waved them aside with an unvarying denial.

This state of affairs was terminated on May 30th. Missouri matters had been watched with intense and daily solicitude at Washington. Each of the Union factions of that State had a spokesman in the Cabinet, Postmaster-General Blair favoring Lyon and his friends, Attorney-General Bates those of Harney; and the President therefore heard the complaints and justifications of both sides. Acting thus on full information, Lincoln, on May 18th, entrusted Frank P. Blair, junior, with a confidential discretionary order to relieve Harney whenever he might deem it necessary. On May 30th, amid the thickening perils from the conspiracy, Blair felt himself justified in acting upon this discretion; Harney was relieved, and Lyon once more placed in command under a newly issued commission as brigadier-general of volunteers, a position to which the first four Missouri regiments had unanimously chosen him.

With Lyon once more in power, the conspirators felt that the crisis of their intrigues had come. Governor Jackson and General Price therefore solicited an interview with the new commander, which being granted, and a safeguard being furnished them, they visited St. Louis on June 11th, and were met by Lyon and Blair, in a conference of several hours' duration. As might have been expected, their views and objects were utterly at variance. The Governor proposed to neutralize Missouri by excluding United States troops and disbanding the Home Guards; Lyon, on the contrary, insisted that the Governor should disband his Missouri militia, and give the Government forces full liberty of movement and control throughout the State. Separating upon these irreconcilable propositions, Governor Jackson and General Price hastened back to Jefferson City that same night, burning the railroad bridges behind them to prevent pursuit; and on the following day, June 12th, the Governor issued a revolutionary proclamation, calling fifty thousand militia into active service to "repel invasion."

Lyon evidently expected little else from the rebellious Governor, for he seems to have been ready with plans and preparations to act against the open insurrection that functionary so defiantly proclaimed. The Missouri River furnished a convenient military highway to the capital of the State; and by the afternoon of June 13th, Lyon had an expedition of three swift river steamers, containing a company of his regulars and several battalions of volunteers, in motion. They arrived before Jefferson City on the 15th of June, landed without opposition, occupied the town, and once more raised the Union flag over the State House. Governor Jackson and his Secretary of State precipitately fled, carrying with them only the great seal of the State, to use in certifying their future publications under the pretended authority of Missouri.

Learning at Jefferson City that the Governor and General Price were gathering a force and preparing to make a stand at Boonville, a town fifty miles farther up the Missouri River, Lyon, on June 16th, the day following his arrival, leaving but a small guard at the capital, again hurriedly embarked his men, numbering about two thousand, and pushed energetically ahead, determined to leave the enemy no time to recruit an army. The steamers passed over the intervening distance during the night, and early next morning (June 17th) Lyon made an unopposed landing four miles below Boonville. The Governor's rallying call had indeed already been responded to by several thousand Missourians, being, however, almost totally without organization, and very poorly armed. Half-way from his landing-place to the town Lyon found a rebel line strongly posted; a spirited fusillade quickly ensued, and for about twenty minutes the Union advance, composed of perhaps five hundred men, was held in check. The enemy could, however, not long withstand the fire of a regular battery which was brought up, and which, with the well-delivered volleys of the better-drilled Union volunteers, soon routed them in a general panic and flight. General Price early retired from Boonville on plea of illness; while Governor Jackson, who viewed the battle from a convenient hill some two miles off, seeing the disastrous result, once more betook himself to flight. Two on the Union, and fifteen on the rebel side, were reported killed, with the usual corresponding number of wounded. Twenty prisoners, two six-pounder guns, two secession flags, and the various supplies of the rebel camp, furnished the Union force substantial trophies of victory. Moving cautiously forward, Lyon occupied the town of Boonville, and issued a quieting proclamation to its terror-stricken inhabitants, while the immature and boyish prisoners he had captured were released on parole. This battle of Boonville ends the administration of Governor Jackson—he had long before forfeited his honor and authority by covert treason; from henceforth his rôle is not only that of an open traitor, but also of a mere fugitive pretender.

The insurrection and flight of the State officers left Missouri without local government. It happened, fortunately, that the State Convention, when in March it took a recess to the following December, empowered a select committee to call it together at any time upon a pressing emergency. The emergency having thus come, the committee issued its call; and the convention, minus some of its disloyal members, but yet having a full constitutional quorum, met once more in Jefferson City, on the 22d of July. It proceeded by ordinance to declare the State offices vacant, to abrogate the Military Bill and other treasonable legislation, and provide for new elections; and finally, on the 31st of July, it elected and inaugurated a provisional government, which thereafter made the city of St. Louis its official headquarters. Hamilton R. Gamble, a Conservative, was made Governor; he announced his unconditional adherence to the Union, and his authority was duly recognized by all those portions of the State which were not under military control of the rebels during the fluctuating fortunes of the local guerilla warfare by which Missouri was so long tormented and desolated.

CHAPTER XI.

KENTUCKY.

THE Alleghany or Appalachian mountain chain, a hundred miles broad and a thousand miles long, extending from New York to Alabama, naturally separated the country into two principal military divisions: that of the East, comprising the Atlantic Coast and the Atlantic States; that of the West, comprising the Mississippi River and its tributaries, and the whole immense territory of the Mississippi Valley. In the East, the line of hostility quickly established itself along the Potomac River, with Washington as its strategical centre; this grew partly out of the paramount necessity of defending the capital, but also largely from the fact that the line from the sea to the mountains was not more than a hundred miles long, and could therefore be occupied and observed without delay. In the West the distance from the mountains to the Mississippi River was nearly ten times as great. This alone would have retarded the definition of the military frontier; but the chief element of uncertainty and delay was furnished by the peculiar political condition of the State of Kentucky, which of itself extends the whole distance from Virginia to Missouri.

It cannot perhaps be affirmed with certainty that Governor Magoffin of Kentucky was a secession conspirator; but his own language leaves no doubt that in opinion and expectation he was a disunionist. He had remonstrated against the rash and separate movements of South Carolina and the Cotton States; but since their movement was made, he looked upon it as final and irrevocable, and committed himself unqualifiedly against coercing them back to obedience. More than this, he argued that Kentucky was no longer safe in the Union, and declared she "will not and ought not to submit to the principles and policy avowed by the Republican party, but will resist, and resist to the death, if necessary."

In this view, he recommended to the Legislature, which met in January under his call, the project of a "Sovereignty" State Convention, appropriations to purchase arms, and the immediate and active organization of the militia. None of these suggestions were, however, adopted by the Legislature, which contented itself for the present by protesting against coercion as unwise and inexpedient, and recommending a call for a national convention. While Kentucky sentiment was deeply pro-slavery, and business and commerce bound her strongly to the South, the patriotic example and teachings of Henry Clay had impressed upon her people a love and reverence for the Union higher and purer than any mere passing interest or selfish advantage.

Nevertheless, as rebellion progressed, the State became seriously agitated and divided. When Sumter fell and the President issued his call for troops, Governor Magoffin insultingly refused compliance. This action in turn greatly excited the people of the three Border Free States of Ohio, Indiana, and Illinois, who thus beheld a not remote prospect of having civil war brought to their own doors. They therefore looked immediately to the protection and control of the Ohio River. Their enthusiastic response to the President's call had filled their capitals with volunteers, which were being armed and equipped by the Government. Ohio hurried off her earliest levies to Cincinnati; those of Indiana were sent to her several exposed river towns. At the extreme southern point of Illinois was the city of Cairo, small in population and commerce, but in a military point of view the commanding centre and key of the whole western river system. Its value was comprehended both east and west. No sooner had the Border Slave State Governors forwarded their disloyal refusals, than Secretary Cameron (April 19th), by telegraph requested the Governor of Illinois to send a brigade of four regiments to occupy it. There was not yet that total of militia in the whole State; but within forty-eight hours an improvised expedition, numbering five hundred and ninety-five men and four six-pounders, started from Chicago to carry out the Secretary's orders, arriving at Cairo on the morning of April 23d, where they were speedily reinforced to the required numbers.

Under the Sumter bombardment, the President's call, and Magoffin's refusal, Kentucky was, for the moment, simply in a hopeless bewilderment, irresolution, and conflict of opinion. A strong minority, arrogating to itself much more than its numerical importance through noise and self-assertion, labored with zeal and energy for secession, but could make no substantial progress against the overwhelming undercurrent of Union sentiment; and these opposing factions, with the ultimate hope of influencing and gaining the wavering or undecided, joined somewhat unavoidably in an endeavor to commit the State to an attitude of strict neutrality.

Governor Magoffin and his personal adherents were ready to lend their official influence to carry the State into rebellion. The Governor sent an agent to the Governors of Arkansas and Louisiana to solicit arms; and by way of justifying the act, he made a similar application to the

Governors of Indiana and of Missouri. No substantial success, however, attended these efforts; and the Governor's application to the banks for money also resulted, in the main, in a discouraging refusal, largely due to the dominating Union sentiment, which suspected him of treasonable designs. A second endeavor to influence the Legislature remained equally barren. That body, which had only adjourned on the 5th of April, was by proclamation once more called to meet in a second special session, beginning May 2d. The Governor's message, reciting the startling events which had occurred, stigmatized the President's defence of the Government as "extraordinary usurpations," the enthusiastic patriotism of the loyal States as "the frenzy of fanaticism," and asserted with dogmatic stubbornness that "the late American Union is dissolved;" recommending, as before, a State convention, military appropriations, and organization of the militia. He also sent a messenger to ask the Governors of Ohio and Indiana to join him "in an effort to bring about a truce between the General Government and the seceded States;" to which Governor Morton worthily responded, "I do not recognize the right of any State to act as mediator between the Federal Government and a rebellious State."

The Unionists had a controlling majority in the Legislature, and, considering the deep agitation and serious divisions in Kentucky, used their power with great moderation and tact, doing as much both to aid the Government and to embarrass the conspirators as was perhaps practicable under the circumstances. To still the prevailing neutrality clamor, the House of Representatives, on May 16th, passed resolutions declaring that Kentucky "should, during the contest, occupy the position of strict neutrality," and also approving Governor Magoffin's refusal to furnish troops. In substan-

9

tial legislation, however, the Governor received little aid or comfort. His most active lieutenant in contemplated treason was Simon B. Buckner, who about a year before had succeeded in obtaining the passage of a rather energetic militia law, under which the Governor appointed him Inspector-General and ranking commander in the State. It was his and the Governor's project to put into the field and manipulate the "State Guard" which this law authorized, so as to precipitate Kentucky into rebellion.

The Legislature, ignoring the Governor's request for a State Convention, addressed itself mainly to the task of turning the influence and support of the militia system from secession to union. A bill was framed and became a law May 24th, authorizing a loan of one million to purchase arms and munitions, but associating a controlling Union Board of Commissioners with the Governor to regulate its disbursement and the distribution of arms; authorizing the formation of Home Guards for local defence; and while it provided that the arms and munitions should not be used against the United States, nor against the Confederate States, unless to protect Kentucky against invasion—it required that both officers and men of the Home Guards and State Guards should alike swear to support the Constitution of the United States and of Kentucky—the former law having required such an oath from the officers alone.

While Kentucky was thus settling down into an attitude of official neutrality, active popular undercurrents were busy in contrary directions. The more ardent secession leaders who raised companies to serve in the field, despairing of obtaining commissions, arms, and active duty from Governor Magoffin, quietly departed to obtain enlistment in the various rebel camps of the South. On the other hand, there were many unconditional Unionists in Kentucky who openly scouted the policy of neutrality, and who from the first were eager that the Government should begin enlistments and gather an armed force to support the Union sentiment in the State. Colonels Guthrie and Woodruff opened a recruiting office on the Ohio side of the river, and as early as May 6th mustered two regiments into service, nominally as the First and Second Kentucky Volunteers, though in reality the men were principally from Ohio and Indiana.

Notwithstanding the contumacious refusals of the Governors of the Border Slave States, President Lincoln was not disposed to give up those States as lost. We have seen that, both in Maryland and Missouri, he authorized direct enlistments under the supervision of United States officers. Leading men having informed him of the actual state of Kentucky sentiment, he, on May 7th, specially commissioned Major Anderson, of Fort Sumter fame, to proceed to Cincinnati and muster into service all loyal volunteers who might offer themselves from Kentucky and West Virginia. Nor was he content with such merely negative encouragement. He felt a deep solicitude to retain Kentucky on the Union side. Very soon also the leading Kentuckians, who at the beginning had been most pertinacious to insist on neutrality, saw that it would be impossible for the State to maintain such an utterly absurd attitude. Mr. Lincoln, therefore, with their knowledge and consent, by the middle of May sent five thousand muskets to Kentucky in charge of Lieutenant William Nelson, and a committee of prominent Union leaders superintended their distribution to companies of loyal Kentucky volunteers which were being secretly formed in various parts of the State; and since this venture proved successful, larger shipments soon followed. As yet all this was done quietly and secretly; for an election was pending in the State, and the Unionists wished to avoid the animosities which open warlike preparations would be sure to create. The elections once over, however, further disguise was thrown off, and at the beginning of July Lieutenant Nelson openly established "Camp Dick Robinson" in Central Kentucky. Into this he quickly gathered several thousand Union volunteers already previously recruited. Before Secessionists or neutral Conservatives were well aware of the fact, he had formed a self-sustaining military post affording a secure rallying-place and support to Kentucky loyalists. Governor Magoffin wrote an official letter to President Lincoln, urging the removal of this and other Union camps from the State; but the President replied that the force was composed exclusively of Kentuckians defending their own homes, and that, in accordance with the evident popular sentiment of the State, he must decline to order them away.

Under these various influences the hopes and schemes of Governor Magoffin and his conspiring secession adherents withered and failed. The "State Guard" of Buckner languished, and the loyal "Home Guards" grew in numbers and effective military strength. So far it had been a contest of quiet, but very earnest political strategy, and the result was in exact conformity to the dominant popular sentiment manifested in the late elections by decisive Union majorities. Sustained by this sentiment, the effort could not well have failed; but failure was rendered impossible, and the result greatly hastened, by the constant presence of a considerable number of Northern troops at Cairo, Cincinnati, and intermediate towns on the border, ready to intervene with active and decisive force, had the necessity at any time become imminent.

Meanwhile surrounding events were rapidly maturing to force Kentucky from her neutral attitude. Not only had hostilities commenced east of the Alleghanies, but active minor campaigns, closing with somewhat important battles, had taken place on each side of Kentucky. Eastward the rebels were driven out of West Virginia with disaster during July; while, to the west, a serious invasion of Missouri was checked in August by the hardy, though over-daring courage of Lyon, who threw back a combined rebel column moving from Arkansas northward, unfortunately at the costly sacrifice of his own life. Unlooked-for success at Bull Run had greatly encouraged the rebellion, but it felt the menace of growing danger in the West. Fremont had been sent to St. Louis, and, with a just pride in his former fame, the whole Northwest was eager to respond to his summons, and follow his lead in a grand and irresistible expedition down the Mississippi River in the coming autumn, which should open the Father of Waters to the Union flag and sever the territory of the Confederacy—a cherished plan of General Scott.

The rebel General Pillow—somewhat wordy, but exceedingly active, and as yet the principal military authority in Tennessee—had long been warning Jefferson Davis to prepare against such an enterprise. He had been working with great energy to fortify Memphis, and, by the middle of May, reported that he would soon have twenty pieces in battery. But at the same time he prophesied that "an effort will be made to effect a lodgment at Columbus, fortify that place, and, with a strong invading column, turn my works, attack them in reverse, crush my supporting force, capture the guns, and open the river. The northern portion of Tennessee is unfavorable, from the extent of open country." He said he had asked Governor Magoffin for permission to fortify Columbus, adding: "If he should withhold his consent, my present impression is that I shall go forward and occupy the work upon the ground of its necessity for protecting Tennessee."

But Jefferson Davis had too great hopes of Kentucky to create enmity by forcing her neutrality, and Pillow's scheme was necessarily postponed. As the autumn approached, however, Kentucky was clearly lost to the "Confederates." Of the members of Congress chosen at the election held June 20th, nine out of ten were loyal. At the general election held on the first Monday of August, the Unionists gained three-fourths of the members of each branch of the Legislature. Meanwhile the danger of a great Mississippi expedition from the North grew formidable. The lower Mississippi flows generally between level shores, and offers few points where the stream may be effectually obstructed by fortifications. It was, therefore, desirable to secure all that were available, and the Richmond authorities now resolved to seize and hold Columbus, notwithstanding the fact that it lay in "neutral" Kentucky.

Since July 4th the defence of the Mississippi River had been specially entrusted to General Leonidas Polk, formerly a bishop in the Protestant Episcopal Church, but who, since the outbreak of the rebellion, preferred to utilize his early West Point education, by laying aside his clerical functions and accepting a major-general's commission in the Confederate service. On September 5th he began moving his forces northward, violating the neutrality of Kentucky by occupying the town of Hickman, on the Mississippi, within that State. The movement did not pass unobserved; the Union commander at Cairo had, with equal vigilance, been studying the possibilities of the river system in his neighborhood. On the following day, Brigadier-General Grant proceeded, with two gunboats and an infantry force, to take possession of the town of Paducah, at the confluence of the

Cumberland and Tennessee Rivers with the Ohio—a movement which bore important fruit a few months later.   General Polk, on his part still marching northward, reached and
occupied Columbus, on the Mississippi, on September 7th.
Having hastily procured the endorsement of this step from
Jefferson Davis, General Polk, on the 9th, formally notified
Governor Magoffin of his presence in Kentucky.

By this time also, the Unionists of the State had completed and compacted their organization and authority, and
demonstrated their strength and predominance.   A new military department, consisting of Kentucky and Tennessee,
and named the Department of the Cumberland, was, on
August 15th, created at Washington and placed under the
command of General Anderson, and since September 1st
that officer had made Louisville his headquarters.   On the
other hand, Buckner had abandoned his professed neutrality
and his militia command, and formally entered the rebel
service as a brigadier-general.   Stationing himself just
within Tennessee, south of Middle Kentucky, he was collect-
ing the rebel members of his "State Guard" for a hostile
expedition against the homes of his former friends and
neighbors.   Another rebel force gathering under Zollicoffer,
in East Tennessee, was watching its opportunity to advance
into Kentucky through Cumberland Gap.

Under these threatening aspects Governor Magoffin communicated to the Legislature, then in session, General Polk's
announcement of his arrival at Columbus.   The altogether
illogical and false rôle of Kentucky neutrality was necessarily at an end.   The Legislature, by express resolutions under
date of September 14th, instructed the Governor to demand
the unconditional withdrawal of the rebel forces from Kentucky, while other resolutions called on General Anderson to
enter at once upon the active defence of his native State.   A

little later, Kentucky still further and finally identified herself with the loyal North.   Enlistment under the Confederate flag was by law declared a misdemeanor, and the invasion of Kentucky by Confederate soldiers a felony, and
heavy punishments were prescribed for both offences.   And
since the Home Guards had only been organized for local
protection, the Legislature now formally authorized the enlistment of forty thousand volunteers to "repel invasion,"
providing that they should be mustered into the service of
the United States, and co-operate with the armies of the
Union.

CHAPTER XII.

PRIOR to 1861, the State of Virginia—the "Old Dominion" —extended from Chesapeake Bay westward to the Ohio River. This broad limit, however, gave her a defective boundary. The Alleghany Mountains, running through the very middle of the State, from northeast to southwest, completely bisected her territory into two divisions somewhat unequal in size, and greatly different in topographical features and character. East of the mountains, the land rises from a broad, low tide-water belt on the sea-coast, in a tolerably regular gradation of plains and plateaus, first to the Blue Ridge, then to the main Appalachian chain; west of the dividing crest, the country retains its mountainous characteristics, a succession of ridges and a medley of hills, till it reaches the Ohio River. Not alone through earlier settlement, but also by reason of climate, soil, and situation, East Virginia remained the region of large plantations, heavy slave population, and profitable agriculture, especially in production of tobacco; West Virginia, on the other hand, became the home of hunters, pioneers, lumbermen, miners, and in latter times the seat of a busy manufacturing industry—developing a diversified agriculture for local consumption, rather than the production of great staples for export. With preponderant population and wealth, East Virginia absorbed political power, and selfishly laid and expended taxes to her local advantage, so that West Virginia was made to stand in the relation of a tributary province, rather than an integral and equally favored part of the commonwealth.

So too grew up essential differences in social tradition and aspiration. The tide-water population developed family estates, pretentious manor-homes, aristocratic exclusiveness, ancestral pride—peculiarities which could not thrive in hunters' camps, or the shanties of miners and lumbermen. The whole world over, and in all ages, mountain and forest life has bred a spirit of self-reliance, of personal independence, of the recognition of individual equality, and rights of simple manhood.

More than anything else, however, the system of slavery antagonized the two sections of the State. By the census of 1860, East Virginia contained 472,494 slaves; while West Virginia, with half as much free population, embraced a total of only 18,371 slaves. It is therefore not surprising that secessionism was rampant in the east, and that unionism prevailed in the west. Of the 55 final votes against the secret Ordinance of Secession in the Virginia Convention, 32 were cast by the West Virginia delegates, 14 others were contributed from other mountain counties; the populous plains and lowlands of the east supplied only 9. As in other parts of the South, the fungus of treason grew rankest in the hot-beds of the heavy slave counties; the poison of conspiracy infected the centres of accumulated wealth, of inherited family pride, of over-fattened political ambition; it was the Tylers, the Wises, the Floyds, the Masons, who, stuffed to repletion with political benefits, turned with ungrateful hearts to destroy the temple of government, wherein as selfish and hypocritical priests they had conducted a dissembling and perverted worship.

While the Convention of Virginia was carrying on its eccentric and fluctuating political intrigues under guise of public deliberation, one of the West Virginia members offered resolutions making a somewhat startling, but entirely germane application of the heretical theory of secession. "The right of revolution," he wrote, "can be exercised as well by a portion of the citizens of a State against their State government, as it can be exercised by the whole people of a State against their Federal Government." "And that any change of the relation Virginia now sustains to the Federal Government, against the wishes of even a respectable minority of her people, would be such an act of injustice perpetrated upon the rights of that minority as to justify them in changing their relation to the State Government by separating themselves from that section of the State that had thus wantonly disregarded their interests and defied their will."

The conspirators in the convention wilfully shut their eyes to the pertinency of this logic, but among the people of West Virginia it remained a quick and pervading principle of action. The Convention at Richmond passed its secret Ordinance of Secession on April 17th; within a week popular movements were already on foot in the towns and populous counties of West Virginia, looking to a division of the State. Numerous causes contributed to this result. Political jealousy and injustice, though a powerful influence, was not everything. Geography had already ordained separation by a formidable mountain-barrier. Her people felt themselves an integral part of the Great West. They responded to the impulse of its commercial ambition, its material development, its expansive business energy. Wheeling aspired to rival Pittsburgh and Cincinnati, not Richmond. They acknowledged neither tobacco nor cotton as kings;

lumber, coal, iron, salt, petroleum, were their candidates
for supremacy in trade. Their commerce followed their
streams into the Ohio. The Mississippi Valley was a
broader market than the Atlantic sea-coast. Their business reached out for St. Louis, St. Paul, and Denver, as
well as Memphis and New Orleans.

The effort, therefore, of the tide-water slaveholding aristo-
crats to carry them into a cotton confederacy, met an in-
stantaneous and almost unanimous protest. The proposition was hardly a subject for discussion. To secede from
secession was the common wish and determination. The
only question was how to put their negative into effective
operation. Rapid popular organization followed; the Government at Washington was appealed to, and promised
countenance and support; and on May 13th, delegates from
twenty-five counties met at Wheeling to consult and devise
further action whereby they might fully and finally repudiate the treasonable revolt of East Virginia.

Circumstances favored their design. Under President
Lincoln's call, the large and populous State of Ohio, West
Virginia's nearest neighbor, was organizing thirteen regi-
ments of three months volunteers. This quota entitled her
to a major-general; and to this important command Gov-
ernor Dennison appointed a young officer of thorough West
Point training and varied experience—Captain George B.
McClellan. He was also a personal favorite of General
Scott, who had such confidence in his ability that he soon
(May 3d) placed him in command of the Military Depart-
ment of the Ohio, created to include the three States of
Ohio, Indiana, and Illinois, with headquarters at Cincin-
nati, and to which West Virginia was not long after attached.
The blockade of Washington, and other incidents, had served
to keep Western quotas of troops on the Ohio line, and the

Unionists of West Virginia thus found a substantial military force at once in their immediate vicinity, with a commanding officer instructed to give them encouragement and support, and carefully studying the possible opportunities of service in their midst.

Although the convention proceedings must have made the Richmond authorities acquainted with the prevailing union sentiment of West Virginia, it is probable that they did not anticipate a general disaffection; not only did Governor Letcher's proclamations for State militia include that section with apparent confidence, but he at an early day despatched officers there to collect and organize it. Relatively, population was sparse and the country mountainous and hilly; there were, therefore, two principal localities, or lines of transit, travel, and business, where concentration could be best effected—one the line of the Baltimore and Ohio Railroad, the other the valley of the Great Kanawha River—and to these districts Governor Letcher sent his agents. Discouraging reports were, however, soon returned: that feeling was very bitter; that union organizations existed in most of the counties; that that section of the State was "verging on actual rebellion." Fragments of rebel companies were indeed here and there springing up, but it became evident that no local force sufficient to hold the country would respond to the Confederate appeal. On the other hand, the open disaffection, and the ominous gathering of forces at several points along the Ohio side of the river, pointed to a short tenure of Confederate authority.

The Richmond officials were, however, unwilling to lose their control without a struggle, and, in default of local military support, determined to maintain themselves with forces from East Virginia. To that end they now sent a few available companies, with some extra arms and supplies, from Staunton at the southern end of the Shenandoah Valley, by the Staunton and Parkersburg turnpike, a tolerably direct route, over the mountains, a distance of seventy-five to a hundred miles to Beverly, from which point they might menace and overawe Grafton, the junction of the main stem of the Baltimore and Ohio Railroad with its branches to Parkersburg and Wheeling.

But the reaction against secession, the reawakening of union feeling, the growth and organization of the party which favored a permanent division of the State, largely outran all the conspirators' efforts and measures. Counter-revolution being positive and aggressive, was not only stronger, but more active than the revolution which had given it birth and opportunity. The inhabitants showed more alacrity to take up arms for the Government than for Letcher and Lee. A West Virginia regiment, formed by Colonel Kelly to fight for the Union, gathered recruits more rapidly at Wheeling, than the rebel camps which Colonel Porterfield had been sent to command and concentrate between Beverly and Grafton.

It will be remembered that the Richmond Convention had appointed the 23d of May (that being also a general election for members of the Legislature) as the day on which the people of Virginia should vote to ratify or reject the Ordinance of Secession. A curiously sophistical and pharisaical argument and appeal, published by Senator Mason in behalf of ratification, shows conclusively that the conspirators were in great apprehension lest their treason should be repudiated at the polls. But, with the State transformed to a camp, and filled with Jefferson Davis' "foreign" regiments, the result could hardly be in doubt. Under complete military domination, East Virginia

voted to ratify; West Virginia, comparatively free, voted to
reject the Secession Ordinance.

This event both justified and sustained the movements
of the West Virginia Unionists and the Government. If
General McClellan had needed any further reasons for an
active military interference, they were furnished by the fact
that Porterfield began burning bridges on the Baltimore
and Ohio Railroad. Realizing that delay was becoming
dangerous, and prompted by directions from Washington,
McClellan, on the 26th, ordered two regiments to cross the
river at Wheeling, and two others at Parkersburg, and to
simultaneously move forward by the branch railroads from
each of these points to their junction at Grafton. Owing to
the necessity of repairing burnt bridges, their progress was
cautious and slow. This gave ample time for Porterfield
to become fully informed of the movement; whereupon
he retired with his small command, stores and spare arms,
to Philippi, on a country road, about fifteen miles directly
south of Grafton, hoping to find there a secure retreat
about which to gather a sufficient force to return and more
thoroughly cut, harass, or control, the railroad.

But the Union forces, being in superior numbers, and as-
sisted with ready information by friendly local sentiment,
gave the rebels little respite. General McClellan had forwarded additional regiments to Grafton, with Brigadier-
General Morris, an educated West Point officer, to command;
and he now adopted and completed an expedition already
projected before his arrival by Colonel Kelly, who, with his
West Virginia regiment, had a thorough knowledge of the
country. Under pretence of an advance on Harper's Ferry,
Colonel Kelly, at the head of about two regiments, started
eastward by rail on the morning of June 2d; that evening a
similar detachment under Colonel Dumont started west-

ward; both columns, however, soon left the cars, and by different roads began a rapid march southward against Philippi. A furious rain-storm during the night greatly impeded,
but also completely concealed, their unexpected advance.
They arrived on opposite hills commanding the town, almost
simultaneously at daylight of June 3d, though, by a mistake
of the proper route, not in a position to cut off retreat.
Here they found Porterfield's command, something over a
thousand strong, carelessly awaiting the arrival of morning
and the abatement of the storm, to begin a retreat which the
rebel officers had informally resolved on the previous evening. The surprise was complete, and the attack so sudden
and sharp as to force the rebels to disperse in utter rout
and disorganization. Their loss in killed and captured was
small, owing to the fatiguing night march which left the
Union troops too thoroughly exhausted to make pursuit.

The complete success of this first dash at the enemy not
only had the happiest effect in inspiriting the Union troops,
but it also encouraged and fortified the West Virginia
Unionists in their political scheme of forming a new State.
On the day after the "Philippi races," as the skirmish was
facetiously nicknamed, a previously concerted agreement to
elect delegates was carried out. These, representing about
forty counties lying between the crest of the Alleghanies and
the Ohio River, met in a formal convention at Wheeling, on
June 11th. Its first step (June 13th), was to repudiate the
treasonable usurpations of the Richmond Convention and
Governor Letcher, to pronounce their acts without authority
and void, and to declare as vacated all executive, legislative,
and judicial offices in the State held by those "who adhere
to said convention and Executive." The second step was
the adoption of an ordinance (June 19th) reorganizing the
State government. On the following day the convention

appointed F. H. Pierpoint Governor, with an advisory council of five, to wield executive authority. A legislature was constituted by calling together, on July 1st, at Wheeling, such members chosen at the election of May 23d as would take a prescribed oath of allegiance to the United States and the restored government of Virginia, and providing for filling the vacancies of those who refused. A similar provision continued or substituted other State and county officers. After adding sundry ordinances of urgent necessity to this groundwork of restoration, the convention on the 25th took a recess till August. The Legislature, however, met according to call, and took up the difficult task of devising legal enactments suitable to the revolutionary crisis; and on July 9th, it chose two United States Senators, who, four days later, were admitted and took part in the national legislation.

So far, the work was simply a repudiation of secession, and a restoration of the usurped government of the whole State. But the main motive and purpose of the counter-revolution was not allowed to halt or fail. In August the Wheeling Convention reassembled, and on the 20th adopted an ordinance creating the new State of Kanawha, and providing for a ratifying popular vote to be taken on the question in the following October. It is not the province of this volume to follow further the political transformation of the "Old Dominion," thus inaugurated, except to add that the proposed "State of Kanawha" became the "State of West Virginia," and was duly admitted to the Union about two years later.

Governor Peirpoint, the head of the provisional government thus organized at Wheeling, made a formal application under the Constitution, to the Government of the United States, for aid to suppress rebellion and protect the

I.—7

people against domestic violence ; and in furtherance of this object General McClellan ordered additional forces into the State from his Department. Local enlistments had also by this time increased West Virginia's own contingent to three regiments under his command. In addition to affording protection to Union sentiment, this military occupation was designed to insure the safety of the Baltimore and Ohio Railroad, not alone of Grafton as a strategical point, but also of the valuable railroad bridge across the Cheat River, and numerous important tunnels in the mountains immediately east of it. The precaution was nowise superfluous ; for the Rebel Government had some weeks before ordered a special expedition to destroy them and permanently break this important line of communication. General Lee still had his eye on such a possibility, and wrote to his new commander, under date of July 1st, " the rupture of the railroad at Cheat River would be worth to us an army."

To effect this, and to hold West Virginia—or at least to prevent the Union forces from penetrating through the mountains in the direction of Staunton—the rebel authorities now sought to repair the Philippi disaster by sending two new commanders to that region : Ex-Governor Henry A. Wise, invested with the rank of brigadier-general, to the Kanawha Valley, and General Garnett, formerly a major in the Federal Army, to Beverly, to gather up and reorganize the débris of Porterfield's command, which they also took immediate measures to reinforce.

Garnett, arriving near the end of June, found that Porterfield had retreated across an outlying mountain range into the Cheat River Valley, in which Beverly is situated. The turnpike from Staunton to Beverly is the central and principal mountain route within a long distance, both to the north and to the south. From Beverly northwestward the turnpike branches, one line going to Buckhannon through a pass over Rich Mountain, the other going to Philippi through a pass in the same range, but which is there named Laurel Hill, the latter being some seventeen miles farther north. " I regard these two passes," wrote Garnett, "as the gates to the northwestern country." Here, then, he proposed to fortify himself, to forage on the country beyond, and to leisurely watch his chance of breaking the railroad. His circumstances were not the most favorable. The troops which he found at Huttonsville on his arrival were " in a miserable condition as to arms, clothing, equipments, instruction, and discipline." " The Union men," he also wrote, "are greatly in the ascendancy here, and are much more zealous and active in their cause than the Secessionists. The enemy are kept fully advised of our movements, even to the strength of our scouts and pickets, by the country people, while we are compelled to grope in the dark as much as if we were invading a foreign and hostile country." Nevertheless, he began a vigorous reorganization ; Lee immediately sent him reinforcements. In a short time he had Colonel Pegram established in the pass at Rich Mountain, with a regiment and six guns, while he himself held the pass at Laurel Hill with three or four regiments, leaving a detachment at Beverly.

This was the situation when, early in July, General McClellan resolved to take the offensive and drive the rebels from West Virginia. He had arrived on the scene of action about the same time with Garnett ; and though he had a largely preponderating force in the State, it was considerably depleted by the local garrisons necessary to protect the railroad, and to give confidence to Unionists in exposed towns. For the immediate work in hand General Morris had five or six regiments at Philippi, confronting Garnett ; McClellan

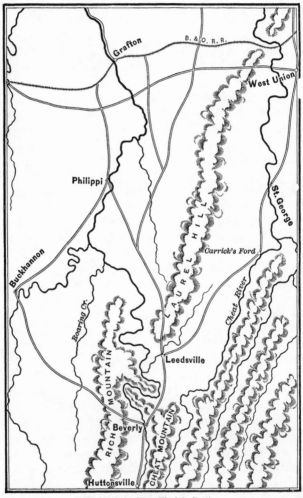

Field of the West Virginia Battles.

directed him to take an advanced position within two miles
of the enemy's works at Laurel Hill, to give an impression
that he intended the main attack, and to be ready to pursue,
should they retreat.

Meanwhile McClellan himself moved to Buckhannon with
some seven regiments, with the design of turning the
enemy's position on Rich Mountain. On the evening of
July 9th he pushed forward to Roaring Creek, two miles
from Pegram's entrenched camp. A reconnoissance on the
10th showed the enemy strongly posted in a mountain defile,
where, with the large force he was supposed to have, a direct
attack in front could only be made at great sacrifice. That
evening Brigadier-General Rosecrans proposed a plan to
turn the position, and McClellan (with some reluctance, it
is said) permitted him to attempt it.

At daylight of July 11th, Rosecrans, with portions of four
regiments—a total of nineteen hundred men—set out, and,
amid a well-nigh continuous rain-storm, by eleven o'clock
cut and climbed their way through a pathless forest and
thicket to the very crest of Rich Mountain. Their ascent
was made south of the turnpike, while Pegram was expecting the attempt on the north. To guard against either contingency, however, as his own camp and entrenchments were
near the west base of the mountain, Pegram had sent a detachment of three hundred and ten men and two guns back
to where the turnpike crosses the summit, two miles in his
rear. There, at the farm of a man named Hart, they had
scarcely had time to throw up some slight entrenchments
for their guns, when Rosecrans' force, advancing toward the
road from the south, encountered them. The rebels made a
plucky resistance, but the Unionists had such advantage in
numbers that the contest was quickly decided. "We formed
at about three o'clock," reports Rosecrans, "under cover of

our skirmishers, guarding well against a flank attack from the direction of the rebels' position, and after a brisk fire which threw the rebels into confusion, carried their position by a charge, driving them from behind some log breastworks, and pursued them into the thickets on the mountain. We captured twenty-one prisoners, two brass six-pounders, fifty stand of arms, and some corn and provisions. Our loss was twelve killed and forty-nine wounded." He also places the reported burials of the rebels killed at one hundred and thirty-five, with about twenty wounded.

McClellan had moved all his force up to Pegram's front, and was waiting to begin a direct assault when he should learn that Rosecrans had commenced the attack on the rear. But Rosecrans' fight on the very top of Rich Mountain disconcerted the arrangement. The messenger sent to communicate between McClellan and himself rode unsuspectingly up to a rebel picket-guard, and was captured. McClellan waited all day in vain for the rear attack to begin; for when the engagement on the mountain was over, the day was already so far advanced, and Rosecrans' men were so thoroughly worn out with their toilsome ascent preceding the fight, that it was deemed most prudent to go into bivouac on the field of battle. McClellan was not informed of the fight and its result until the following day, July 12th, when it was also ascertained that the whole rebel camp and position had been precipitately evacuated; he was therefore now able, not only to secure their abandoned guns and supplies, but to push without opposition along the turnpike entirely over the mountain and occupy Beverly.

Pegram had, on the 11th, personally gone to the mountain-top—only, however, to witness the defeat and dispersion of his little detachment. Seeing himself thus in a trap, with McClellan in front and Rosecrans in secure possession of the road behind him, he returned to his camp, and spiking his four guns, abandoned his camp and equipage and undertook to escape, with the remainder of his command—about six hundred men—by marching northward along the mountain to join Garnett at Laurel Hill. For the moment he succeeded in eluding both the Federal commanders, and after a laborious eighteen hours' march over an almost impassable route, found himself within three miles of Leedsville. Here, however, he received news that Garnett had also retreated, and that a strong Union column was in pursuit. Thus he was once more caught between two Union armies ; and seeing no further avenue of escape, he that night, July 12th, sent a proposal of surrender to General McClellan, who, on the following morning (July 13th), received Pegram and his command, a total remainder of five hundred and sixty men and thirty-three officers, as prisoners of war, at Beverly, where the half-famished rebel fugitives were only too glad to once more receive comfortable quarters and rations.

The earliest fugitives who escaped from the battle of Rich Mountain, on the afternoon of July 11th, carried the news of that disaster to Beverly, enabling the rebel regiments stationed there to retreat southward, and also, as is probable, communicating the intelligence to Garnett at Laurel Hill. That officer, already seriously threatened by General Morris in his immediate front, thereupon perceived that his position was no longer tenable, and ordered an immediate retreat. When Garnett reached Leedsville on the afternoon of the 12th, and heard that McClellan was at Beverly, he saw that his own further retreat to the south was also cut off. There was now no resource left but to adopt the rather desperate alternative of turning to the north and attempting to reach St. George and West Union by a rough and difficult mountain road. His command of thirty-three hundred men and cumbrous trains thereby necessarily became very much scattered and disorganized. Although he had some fifteen hours the start of the Union pursuit, an advance column of three Federal regiments, led by Captain Benham of the Engineers, gained rapidly on the fugitives. Notwithstanding every effort of the rebels to impede them by felling trees in the narrow mountain defiles, the Union advance came up with their wagon-train at Carrick's Ford, one of the crossings of Cheat River, twenty-six miles northwest of Laurel Hill, about noon of July 13th. Here Garnett in person faced about his rear-guard (a single regiment, according to the rebel report), and taking post on a favorable and precipitous elevation of the right river bank, fifty to eighty feet high, planted three guns to command the ford and approaching road, and prepared to defend his retreat.

Steedman's regiment, with two guns, was leading the Union advance, and came up on the low, narrow approach, within close musket-range, before they discovered the rebel line. A brisk engagement at once ensued, and the other two regiments soon arrived. Owing to the restricted space, Milroy's regiment was obliged to take position where it could only deliver an oblique fire and at a greater distance. Dumont's regiment was thereupon ordered to advance and scale a difficult height in order to turn the enemy's left flank. Two companies had well-nigh gained the coveted position, when Benham received a mistaken report that the ascent was impracticable. He therefore ordered Dumont to return, to march his regiment along the very base of the hill on which the rebels were posted, to their right flank, and make the ascent there. The manœuvre was gallantly executed, and scarcely had Dumont begun mounting the height, when the rebel line broke and fled, abandoning one of their guns.

Retreat and pursuit were once more commenced; and at

the next ford, perhaps a quarter of a mile farther on, there occurred an interchange of desultory skirmish-fire between small parties of sharpshooters, in which Garnett himself was killed.

At this result the Federals abandoned further pursuit, satisfied with the capture of the baggage-train, one gun, two stands of colors, and fifty prisoners; the casualties being thirteen killed and forty wounded of the Federals, and twenty killed and ten wounded of the rebels. McClellan had ordered yet another column to be gathered up along the railroad to intercept the flying enemy at West Union; but no substantial result followed the effort, and the remainder of Garnett's command escaped.

Counted according to mere numbers, the battles of Rich Mountain and Carrick's Ford fall into a ridiculous insignificance in contrast with the great battles of the rebellion during the next three years. Hundreds of engagements, of greater magnitude and much more serious loss of life, preceded or followed the main contests of the war, of which history will hardly make a note. But this petty skirmish with three hundred rebels on Rich Mountain, and this rout of a little rear-guard at Carrick's Ford, were speedily followed by large political and military results. They closed a campaign, dispersed a rebel army, recovered a disputed State, permanently pushed back the military frontier. They enabled McClellan to send a laconic telegram, combining in one report * the scattered and disconnected incidents of

---

* "HUTTONSVILLE, VA., July 14, 1861.

"COLONEL TOWNSEND:

"Garnett and forces routed; his baggage and one gun taken; his army demoralized; Garnett killed. We have annihilated the enemy in Western Virginia, and have lost thirteen killed, and not more than forty wounded. We have in all killed at least two hundred of the enemy, and their prisoners will amount to at

three different days and happening forty miles apart, which (without exaggerating literal truth except as to the Union losses and number of prisoners) gave such a general impression of professional skill and achievement as to make him the hero of the hour, and which started a train of circumstances that, without further victories, made him General-in-Chief of all the Armies of the United States, on the first day of November following.

McClellan's campaign in West Virginia ends with the death of Garnett and the dispersion of his army. About a week afterward he was called to a new field of duty at Washington City. There is not room in this volume to further describe military operations in West Virginia during the remainder of the year 1861. Various movements and enterprises occurred under command of Wise, Floyd, and Lee, on the rebel side; and under Cox, Rosecrans, Milroy, and other gallant officers of the Union army. With somewhat fluctuating changes, the rebels were gradually forced back out of the Great Kanawha Valley; and the aggregate result left West Virginia in possession of the Federal troops, her own inherent loyalty having contributed largely to this condition. The union sentiment of the people was everywhere made more and more manifest, and the new State government was consolidated and heartily sustained, ending, as has already been mentioned, by her ultimate admission as a separate member of the Federal Union, in June, 1863.

---

least one thousand. Have taken seven guns in all. I still look for the capture of the remnant of Garnett's army by General Hill. The troops defeated are the crack regiments of Eastern Virginia, aided by Georgians, Tennesseeans, and Carolinians. Our success is complete, and secession is killed in this country.

"GEO. B. McCLELLAN,

"Major-General Commanding."

CHAPTER XIII.

PATTERSON'S CAMPAIGN.

UNDER the President's three months call the State of Pennsylvania was required to furnish sixteen regiments. This entitled her to two major-generals, and one of these, appointed by the Governor, was Robert Patterson. He had served with credit as a lieutenant and captain in the war of 1812, and as a major-general in the Mexican War; General Scott regarded him as "an excellent second in command;" his selection seemed, therefore, natural and proper. Notwithstanding he had now reached the age of sixty-nine, he entered at once with alacrity on the task of organizing the three months volunteers in the city of Philadelphia. After the Baltimore riot and the Maryland uprising, it became necessary to create the military "Department of Pennsylvania," comprising Pennsylvania, Delaware, and part of Maryland, and Patterson was assigned to its command, with directions to co-operate in restoring Union authority in Maryland.

Sundry joint military movements projected to accomplish this object, were happily soon rendered unnecessary by the rapid accumulation of troops at Washington, Butler's occupation of Baltimore, and the sweeping political reaction in Maryland. But, meanwhile, the rebels had established a strong camp at Harper's Ferry, and Patterson's close attention was thus very naturally transferred to that point. The three months troops could not be used in distant undertakings. Here, however, was a worthy enterprise at the very threshold of Pennsylvania, which, successfully prosecuted, would protect Maryland, relieve the Baltimore and Ohio Railroad, encourage Virginia Unionists, and recover lost prestige. Patriotic pride, political security, and military advantage seemed, to the minds of both Patterson and Scott, to present combined reasons for an early recapture of Harper's Ferry.

For this purpose, Patterson, about the first of June, concentrated his available troops at Chambersburg, Pa., and on the third of that month issued an address to the regiments under his command, announcing that "you will soon meet the insurgents." Orders from General Scott, however, held him back until strong reinforcements could be sent, and an important diversion organized to aid him; and while thus assisting, the General also admonished him to every prudence, reminding him that his expedition was "well projected, and that success in it would be an important step in the war; but, there must be no reverse."

With the increase of his force, and a closer survey of his task, Patterson's own estimate of his enterprise grew in magnitude. "Remember, I beseech you," he wrote to the Secretary of War, under date of June 10th, "that Harper's Ferry is (as I have said from the first) the place where the first great battle will be fought, and the result will be decisive of the future. The insurgents are strongly intrenched, have an immense number of guns, and will contest every inch of ground. . . . . The importance of a victory at Harper's Ferry cannot be estimated. I cannot sleep for thinking about it. . . . . I beseech you, therefore, by our ancient friendship, give me the means of success. You have the means; place them at my disposal, and shoot me if I do not use them to advantage."

With such professions of a fighting spirit, the Administration looked with some confidence for an offensive campaign, and sent its best regiments and officers to take part in it. Both General Scott and General Patterson were, however, deceived in their expectation that the rebels meant to risk a battle at that point. With a total force of something over seventeen regiments, Patterson at length began his forward movement via Hagerstown and Williamsport. But so leisurely were his preparations and advance, that the rebels had every knowledge of his coming; and when, on June 15th, he finally reached the Potomac River, he found, instead of the "desperate resistance" which had been looked for, that Johnston had hastily evacuated Harper's Ferry after destroying the railroad bridge and spiking his heavy guns, and had retreated upon Winchester.

Patterson and his officers were greatly mystified by this withdrawal of the enemy. "I believe it is designed for a decoy," wrote Fitz John Porter, Chief of Staff, to Cadwalader, second in command. "There may be a deep-laid plot to deceive us." "The whole affair is to me a riddle," wrote Cadwalader back to Porter. Advancing with a painful overcaution, as if Johnston were the invader, a part of the army crossed the Potomac on the 16th of June.

Finding the rumor of the evacuation true, Patterson took sufficient courage to report a victory. "They have fled, and in confusion," he wrote. "Their retreat is as demoralizing as a defeat; and, as the leaders will never be caught, more beneficial to our cause. Harper's Ferry has been retaken without firing a gun."

"What movement, if any, in pursuit of the enemy, do you propose to make, consequent on the evacuation of Harper's Ferry?" asked General Scott by telegraph. "Design no pursuit; cannot make it," replied Patterson. That deter-

mination necessarily ended this first part of the campaign;
and General Scott thereupon ordered the extra reinforcements back to Washington.

If the evacuation of Harper's Ferry was a mystery to Patterson, it was a plain and common-sense necessity to the
rebel commander. Occasionally an idea finds a tenacious and
almost ineradicable lodgment in the public mind, without
a shadow of reason or truth to justify it. Because the fan-
atic John Brown selected Harper's Ferry as the scene of his
wild exploit, the public mind jumped to the conclusion that
that spot was a natural stronghold, a Gibraltar, a Thermopylæ. Now, the single mountain-line called the Blue Ridge,
crossing the Potomac River at Harper's Ferry, is as far from
being a mountain stronghold as a straight line of picket-
fence across a brook is from being a block-house. John
Brown was as unsound in war as in politics. But it would
seem that, even in highly civilized nations, there lingers a
remnant of the savage superstition that insanity is inspiration; for strong minds caught at the suggestion that he had
recognized in Harper's Ferry a negro Thermopylæ.

This was apparently the light in which the rebel authorities regarded the place, and its occupancy and retention was
made a prime object at the beginning. Jefferson Davis himself sent Johnston, one of his best officers, to command it.
"My conversations with General Lee, in Richmond," says
Johnston, "and the President's [Jefferson Davis] oral instructions to me in Montgomery, had informed me distinctly
that they regarded Harper's Ferry as a natural fortress, commanding the entrance into the Valley of Virginia from Pennsylvania and Maryland, and that it was occupied in that idea,
and my command not that of a military district and active
army, but of a fortress and its garrison."

When Johnston arrived, however, and made a personal in-

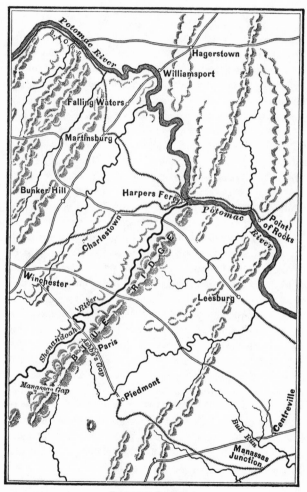

Patterson's Campaign.

spection of the neighborhood, he at once recognized the error of this assumption. "There is no danger of attack in front," he wrote (May 26th), "but the position is easily turned by crossing the river above or below. The present force is not sufficient for defence against a superior one attacking from the Virginia side. Relief, in case of investment, could not be furnished. Considered as a position, I regard Harper's Ferry as untenable against a strong enemy. We have outposts at the Point of Rocks, near the ferry at Williamsport, and the bridge at Shepherdstown, the extreme points being at least thirty miles apart." Two days later he repeated his statement, his engineer reporting that "to hold this post, then, either as a fortress, a *point d'appui*, or as a condition of the defence of the Virginia Valley, we require a force of from twelve to fifteen thousand men."

Lee did not relish the alternative; he sent him two additional regiments, and wrote him that the abandonment of Harper's Ferry "would be depressing to the cause of the South." But Johnston held stubbornly to his opinion, and wrote on June 6th, that, though the abandonment of Harper's Ferry might be depressing to the cause of the South, the loss of five or six thousand men would be more so. "And if they remain here," he added, "they must be captured or destroyed very soon after General McClellan's arrival in the valley." The opinion was evidently based on the current rumors that McClellan would bring Western troops to join Patterson.

This decided warning had its effect on the rebel authorities, and under date of June 13th they authorized Johnston to retire upon Winchester, after destroying everything at Harper's Ferry, "whenever the position of the enemy shall convince you that he is about to turn your position." But they coupled the permission with another strong reminder:

" The position of Harper's Ferry, as has been heretofore
stated, is deemed valuable because of its relation to Maryland and as the entrance to the Valley of Virginia, the possession of which by the enemy will separate the eastern and
western sections of the State from each other, deprive us of
the agricultural resources of that fertile region, and bring in
its train political consequences which it is well believed you
cannot contemplate without the most painful emotions."
With Patterson on the point of moving against him, however, Johnston allowed political consequences to take care of
themselves, destroyed Harper's Ferry on June 13th and 14th,
and retired even before his permission was received. " We
are twelve miles in advance of Winchester," he reported on
the 17th ; " my only hope from this movement is a slight
delay in the enemy's advance. I believe his force to be
about eighteen thousand ; ours is six thousand five hundred."
Patterson admits that he had seventeen regiments—a force
fully capable of the brilliant and important blow he had
been ambitious to strike, but which he had neither the skill
nor courage to direct.

The succeeding two weeks furnish no incidents worthy of
note in this connection. Practically the two armies re-
mained in observation, inactive, and without definite plans.
When General Scott withdrew the temporary reinforcements
he had given Patterson to enable him to fight a battle, the
latter once more retired to the north bank of the Potomac.
For the moment military attention was directed elsewhere.
McClellan was preparing his campaign in West Virginia ;
McDowell was strengthening the Federal occupation of
Arlington Heights and Alexandria; the President and
General Scott were deliberating upon possible operations
against Manassas. In this interim Johnston remained in
camp about Winchester, pushing his picket-line close up

11

to the Potomac, and keeping himself well informed by scouts and spies. Meanwhile the Confederate authorities, still anxious to hold the Shenandoah Valley, and having also in view a possible junction with Beauregard at Manassas, sent forward reinforcements which raised Johnston's army to the effective strength of nine thousand, besides twenty-five hundred local militia in process of organization.

Toward the end of June a movement against Manassas was resolved on at Washington. As a preliminary, General Scott once more suggested a definite task to Patterson. "Remain in front of the enemy," he telegraphed on June 25th, "while he continues in force between Winchester and the Potomac. If you are in superior or equal force, you may cross and offer him battle." Two days later he gave further emphasis to the suggestion by saying, "I had expected your crossing the river to-day in pursuit of the enemy." But Patterson complained that Johnston outnumbered him, and clamored for reinforcements and batteries. Reinforcements and batteries were ordered to join him, and he was also informed of the intended movement on Manassas ; upon which he again put on a bold front and crossed the Potomac at Williamsport, moving to Martinsburg, with sufficient opposition to bring on a smart skirmish at Falling Waters, the enemy retiring toward Winchester as he advanced.

From this point, during the short time he yet remained in command, Patterson's military conduct becomes the subject of criticism and controversy. It is military usage—perhaps military necessity establishes the usage—that orders and directions from superior to subordinate officers are conveyed in brief words expressing or suggesting only the objects to be accomplished, and leaving methods largely at the discretion of him who has to perform the task. Following this established usage, General Scott, by his orders and directions from July 1st to the 13th, informed Patterson that McDowell would make an advance against Beauregard, and that Johnston must be defeated or detained in the Shenandoah Valley, in order that their two armies might not unite and defeat McDowell. "I telegraphed to you yesterday," was Scott's language, "if not strong enough to beat the enemy early next week, make demonstrations so as to detain him in the valley of Winchester; but if he retreats in force toward Manassas, and it be too hazardous to follow him, then consider the route via Key's Ferry, Leesburg, etc." That Patterson correctly understood the order is shown by his reply: "I have thus far succeeded in keeping in this vicinity the command under General Johnston, who is now pretending to be engaged in fortifying at Winchester, but prepared to retire beyond striking distance if I should advance too far. To-morrow I advance to Bunker Hill preparatory to the other movement. If an opportunity offers, I shall attack; but, unless I can rout, shall be careful not to set him in full retreat upon Strasburg."

But the wishes of the Administration and General Scott were not allowed to depend alone on the customary orders. Patterson's former indecision and hesitancy had created a doubt of his disposition to fight; and a similar hesitancy was once more manifesting itself in his complaints, requests, and especially in his growing exaggeration of his antagonist's strength. It is always deemed hazardous to change commanders on the eve of battle, and therefore the alternative was adopted of sending General Sandford to him with additional reinforcements; who, waiving his rank, should take command under Patterson, and prompt him in pushing forward the army. Sandford, accepting the duty, reported to Patterson with four regiments from Washington, about July 10th; the independent column under General Stone also joined him immediately afterward, so that Patterson's army now numbered eighteen thousand two hundred according to his own estimate, or over twenty-two thousand according to the estimate of others, opposed to the rebel army, which, altogether, Johnston states to have been less than twelve thousand men.

It would appear that at this time two impulses struggled for mastery in Patterson's mind. Apparently he was both seeking and avoiding a battle. He had called a council of war at Martinsburg on the 9th; and verifying the military adage that a council of war never fights, his officers had advised him that he was on a "false line," and that he could most advantageously threaten Johnston from Charlestown. Accordingly, on July 12th, Patterson asked permission to transfer his forces to that line; while a dispatch from General Scott of the same date, in reply to a former letter, in substance accorded him the permission, but accompanied it with the significant reminder: "Consider this suggestion well, and except in an extreme case do not recross the Potomac with more than a sufficient detachment for your supplies on the canal."

Such a movement upon Charlestown, made promptly at that date and under the then existing conditions, might have been judicious. But Patterson's dispatches show that from this on he found nothing but reasons for fear and justification for inaction and retreat. He wanted a regiment of regulars; he said the time of the three months regiments was about to expire; that his men were barefooted; that the enemy was reinforced and fortified; that "to attack under such circumstances, against the greatly superior force at Winchester, is most hazardous."

Under these renewed manifestations of timidity General Scott's patience began to give way, and he now sent Patterson two prompting telegrams, which ought to have warmed the sluggish blood of even sixty-nine years to action. " Do not let the enemy amuse and delay you with a small force in front," he telegraphed July 17th, "whilst he reinforces the [Manassas] Junction with his main body. McDowell's first day's work has driven the enemy beyond Fairfax Court House. The Junction will probably be carried to-morrow." And again on the following day : " I have certainly been expecting you to beat the enemy. If not, to hear that you had felt him strongly, or, at least, had occupied him by threats and demonstrations. You have been at least his equal, and I suppose superior in numbers. Has he not stolen a march and sent reinforcements toward Manassas Junction? A week is enough to win victories." Unfortunately, Patterson, even before he received the first of these, had already committed the fatal military blunder of a retreat. But the questions were so searching, and so plainly conveyed a reprimand, that he replied in a tone of offended dignity : "The enemy has stolen no march upon me. I have kept him actively employed, and, by threats and reconnoissances in force, caused him to be re-enforced. I have accomplished in this respect more than the General-in-Chief asked, or could well be expected in face of an enemy far superior in numbers, with no line of communication to protect." The answer was admirable in form and spirit, but it lacked the essential element of correctness. The enemy did not outnumber him—was, in fact, only two-thirds as strong—and was at that moment actually making a rapid " stolen march " to Manassas, which Patterson did not discover till two days afterward.

Understanding fully, both from General Scott's telegrams and General Sandford's personal explanations, that an advance against Manassas Junction was in progress, which would lead to a heavy battle between McDowell and Beauregard, Patterson had moved from Martinsburg on July 15th, directly toward Johnston at Winchester, as far as Bunker Hill, within nine miles of the enemy. On the following day he ordered a slight reconnoissance. Until the night of the 16th it was believed by his officers that the advance meant fight. Every one understood that the critical moment had come, or was at hand. The time for elaborate strategy or new combinations had passed. Confronting the enemy there were but three alternatives admissible under his imperative duty : to hold him, to fight him, or to follow him.

It is sad to relate that, with the complete advantage of numbers and position, he did neither. In justice to him, however, it should always be remembered that his personal instinct was right, and that he was led into his fatal error mainly by the influence of his chief-of-staff, Fitz John Porter. His senior aid-de-camp, in his testimony before the Committee on the Conduct of the War, relates the circumstances under which he took his final decision :

"At one time, General Patterson had given an order to move from Bunker Hill to Winchester. He was very unwilling to leave Johnston, even at Winchester, without attacking him ; and on the afternoon before we left Bunker Hill he decided to attack him, notwithstanding his strong force.

"Question. Behind his intrenchments ?

"Answer. Yes, sir ; it went so far that his order was written by his assistant adjutant-general, Colonel Porter. It was very much against the wishes of Colonel Porter, and he asked General Patterson if he would send for Colonel Abercrombie and Colonel Thomas, and consult them on the movement. General Patterson replied : ' No, sir ; for I know they will attempt to dissuade me from it, and I have made up my mind to fight Johnston under all circumstances.' That was the day before we left Bunker Hill. Then Colonel Porter asked to have Colonel Abercrombie and Colonel Thomas sent for and consulted as to the best manner to carry out his wishes. He consented, and they came, and after half an hour they dissuaded him from it."

With his intentions thus changed, Patterson late that night ordered a retrograde movement; and the next day, July 17th, his army marched to Charlestown—nominally as a flank movement, but practically in retreat, since it about doubled the distance between himself and the enemy. It adds neither excuse nor credit to himself or his advising subordinates that, as a partial justification, they had gulped down an absurd rumor about the enemy being forty thousand strong, without taking any efficient means to ascertain its correctness. And so lifeless and inefficient had the whole army become under such influences and management, that not till July 20th did Patterson learn the humiliating fact that he had wrecked the fair military reputation of a lifetime by permitting the enemy to escape through utterly inexcusable lack of energy and want of judgment. And if that reflection could be still further embittered, it was done by the early realization that his stupendous blunder had lost to the Union cause the first important battle of the war.

Johnston was at Winchester, in daily anticipation of Patterson's attack, when, a little after midnight of July 17th, he received orders from the Confederate authorities to go at once to the help of Beauregard. Just twenty-four hours had elapsed since Patterson's order to retreat, and the Union army was already at Charlestown. By nine o'clock on the morning of July 18th, Johnston's scouts brought him reports indicating clearly the actual situation. At noon of that day he had his whole effective force of nine thousand men on the march; at nightfall his advance passed through Ashby's

Gap of the Blue Ridge; by eight o'clock on the 19th it was at Piedmont, the nearest station of the Manassas Gap Railroad, and embarking here in cars, seven regiments were in Beauregard's camp, at Manassas, that afternoon. Johnston himself, with another detachment, arrived at Manassas at noon of Saturday, July 20th; and most of the remainder of his force reached the battle-field of Bull Run in the nick of time to take a decisive part in that famous conflict, about three o'clock on Sunday, July 21st. It was these nine thousand men of Johnston's army which not merely decided, but principally fought the battle. Patterson could and ought either to have defeated or held them at Winchester. Only a little more than a month had elapsed since he had written to the Secretary of War, "Give me the means of success. You have the means; place them at my disposal, and shoot me if I do not use them to advantage." He would have fared ill under a literal enforcement of his own offer.

CHAPTER XIV.

MANASSAS.

On the 23d of May, 1861, according to the conspirators' programme, Virginia was put through the dumb show of indorsing the Secession Ordinance by a nominal popular vote; and almost immediately thereafter, about June 1st, the Confederate seat of government was transferred from Montgomery to Richmond. The reasons for this course were palpable; it gratified the local pride of the Old Dominion secessionists; it gave the reins of local military domination definitely into Jefferson Davis' personal grasp; it placed him on the most advantageous frontier to meet the expected Union advance from Washington. This, as previously related, had already seized upon Alexandria and Arlington Heights, which were now being extensively fortified. Making a short speech to a serenade on the evening of June 1st, the rebel chief announced that Virginia was "to become the theatre of a great central camp, from which will pour forth thousands of brave hearts to roll back the tide of this despotism."

The local campaign had already taken shape before his arrival. Since Lee was placed in command he had followed a policy which looked less to the capture of Baltimore than to the obstruction of the Potomac. His first and principal task had been to organize the volunteers which Gover-

nor Letcher called into service; and the earliest levies of
Northern Virginia were posted at Manassas Junction, where
railroads from Richmond, from Alexandria, and from the
Shenandoah Valley met.   On examination, its strategical
value was found to be much greater than was suspected at
the beginning; Colonel Cocke, the local commander, first
pointed out to Lee its important relation to the Shenandoah
Valley.   "These two columns," he writes, under date of May
15th, "one at Manassas and one at Winchester, could readily
co-operate and concentrate upon the one point or the other,
either to make head against the enemy's columns advancing
down the valley, should he force Harper's Ferry; or, in case
we repulse him at Harper's Ferry, the Winchester supporting column could throw itself on this side of the mountains,
to co-operate with the column at Manassas."

With the great increase of Federal troops at Washington,
and their seizure of Alexandria and Arlington Heights, the
post at Manassas Junction became of such prominence and
importance, that Beauregard was sent to take command of it
about June 1st.   Beauregard was an officer of curiously unequal merit : thoroughly educated, and highly skilful in the
science and art of military engineering, he had little capacity
for administration, or sound judgment in the conception of
large field-operations.   Giddy to intoxication with laudation
for his cheap victory at Sumter, he now invited upon his
own head the contempt of the world, and of history, by pub-
lishing a proclamation in which, without provocation, he
charged the Union armies to have abandoned " all rules of
civilized warfare," and to have made " Beauty and Booty "
their war-cry.   His next exploit was to excite the distrust of
the Richmond authorities upon his military ability, by pro-
posing a series of aggressive movements intended to annihi-
late the Union armies and capture Washington ; liable, how-

ever, to the objection, noted thereon by Jefferson Davis, that "the plan was based on the improbable and inadmissible supposition that the enemy was to await everywhere, isolated and motionless, until our forces could effect junctions to attack them in detail." Meanwhile he rendered his superiors a real service in pointing out that the defence of his position should be made, not with earthworks at Manassas, but with troops on the line of Bull Run, and for this he was urgent in demanding large reinforcements.

As has been already mentioned, it was General Scott's opinion that the Government ought not to engage in any military undertakings with the three months volunteers, beyond those to which these forces had been already assigned and distributed, namely: to protect Washington and fortify Arlington Heights ; to garrison Fort Monroe and, if chance should offer, recapture the Gosport Navy Yard at Norfolk ; to hold Baltimore and Maryland ; to prosecute Patterson's campaign against Harper's Ferry ; to recover West Virginia through McClellan's campaign ; to guard the Ohio line, and control Kentucky and Missouri. Larger and more distant operations, he believed, ought to be undertaken only with new armies formed of the three years volunteers, giving the summer to drill and preparation, and entering on combined movements in the favorable autumn weather.

Important reasons, partly military, partly political, conflicted with so deliberate a programme. As events had shaped themselves, it seemed necessary to aid Patterson. The possibility that Beauregard and Johnston might unite their armies was clearly enough perceived ; hence, a column to threaten Manassas was proposed. Indications were also manifesting themselves that rebel batteries at narrow places might soon seriously embarrass the navigation of the Potomac. Chiefly, however, the highly excited patriotism of the

North, eager to wipe out national insult and vindicate national authority, was impatient of what seemed tedious delay. The echoes of the Sumter bombardment were yet in the air; the blood on the Baltimore paving-stones was crying loudly to heaven. For half a century the nation had felt no close experience of war. The conquests of peace had grown almost miraculous in speed and certainty. Rivers and mountains, distance and time, had become the obedient ministers of creative ingenuity and bold enterprise. Forgetting that the achievements of peace encountered the opposing obstacles, not of man, but of nature alone, the North demanded speedy as well as signal redress. It saw rebellion enthroned in the capital of Virginia; it saw a numerous Union army gathered at Washington; the newspapers raised the cry of "On to Richmond;" and the popular heart beat in quick and well-nigh unanimous response to the slogan. Latterly a detachment sent out by General Butler from Fortress Monroe had met a repulse at Great Bethel, and near Washington a railroad-train under General Schenck had run into an ambush at Vienna station; both were trifling losses, but at the moment supremely irritating to the pride of the North, and the fires of patriotic resentment once more blazed up with fresh intensity.

General Scott's first project of an expedition against Manassas was made about the beginning of June, the object then being not to fight a battle, but merely make a threatening diversion to aid Patterson. There were at that time only some six thousand rebels at Manassas, according to Beauregard's report. Before the design could take final shape, Johnston had evacuated Harper's Ferry, and Patterson's first movement was thereby terminated. This occurred about the middle of June.

From that time on, the plan grew into the idea of a larger

and more decisive movement. Beauregard was receiving large reinforcements; nevertheless, the strength of the Union army at Washington was such that it seemed entirely possible to provide every chance of success. McDowell, raised in rank from the grade of major to that of brigadier-general, and placed in command at Arlington Heights, submitted a formal plan, at the request of the General-in-Chief, about June 24th. His plan assumed that the secession forces at Manassas and its dependencies would number twenty-five thousand; that they would unavoidably become apprised of the movement, and every effort would be made to increase Beauregard's strength; but that "if General J. E. Johnston's force is kept engaged by Major-General Patterson, and Major-General Butler occupies the force now in his vicinity (Fortress Monroe), I think they will not be able to bring up more than ten thousand men." Against such an array he proposed to move with a force of thirty thousand of all arms, and a reserve of ten thousand.

The project was elaborately discussed, and finally agreed upon, at a council of war at the Executive Mansion, on June 29th, in which President Lincoln, his Cabinet, and the principal military officers took part. As already mentioned, General Scott was opposed to the undertaking; but, after it was once resolved upon, he joined with hearty good-will in every effort to make it a success. McDowell was emphatic in his protest that he could not hope to beat the combined armies of Johnston and Beauregard; upon which Scott gave him the distinct assurance: "If Johnston joins Beauregard, he shall have Patterson on his heels." With this understanding, the movement was ordered to begin a week from that day.

The enterprise did not escape the usual fate of unforeseen delay; it marks great energy in McDowell that his expedition was only deferred a little over a week beyond the appointed time. On the 16th of July he issued his orders to march that afternoon. His army was organized as follows:

First Division, commanded by TYLER: an aggregate of 9,936 men, divided into four brigades, respectively under Keyes, Schenck, Sherman, and Richardson.

Second Division, commanded by HUNTER: an aggregate of 2,648 men, divided into two brigades, under Porter and Burnside.

Third Division, commanded by HEINTZELMAN: an aggregate of 9,777 men, divided into three brigades, under Franklin, Willcox, and Howard.

Fourth Division, commanded by RUNYON: an aggregate of 5,752 men; no brigade commanders.

Fifth Division, commanded by MILES: an aggregate of 6,207 men, divided into two brigades, under Blenker and Davies.

Thus, the total of his command, not including four regiments left in the Alexandria and Arlington forts, was 34,320 men. From this number, however, Runyon's division may at once be deducted; it was left behind to guard his communications, its most advanced regiment being seven miles in rear of Centreville. McDowell's actual moving column may therefore be said to have consisted of 28,568 * men, including artillery, a total of forty-nine guns, and a single battalion of cavalry.

---

* From this number it is entirely just to make yet another deduction. The period of enlistment of the Fourth Pennsylvania Regiment, and of Captain Varian's Battery of (New York) Light Artillery having expired, they were discharged by official order at Centreville, July 20th, the day before the battle.

It will thus be seen. that, instead of the thirty thousand he asked for, McDowell had, perhaps, less than twenty-eight thousand men, with forty-nine guns; and official reports show that, instead of the thirty-five thousand rebels he expected to meet at Manassas, there were on the field thirty-two thousand men, with fifty-seven guns—less than his estimate, but about four thousand more than his own army.

Of all machines, an army develops, perhaps, the greatest inefficiency from mere friction, or the greatest usefulness from action and thoroughness of organization. The value of a veteran consists as much of his habitual expertness in the routine of camp and march, as of coolness and confidence under fire. Two principal causes rendered the advance very slow. The first was the want of practice in marching. "They stopped every moment to pick blackberries or get water," says McDowell; "they would not keep in the ranks, order as much as you pleased; when they came where water was fresh, they would pour the old water out of their canteens, and fill them with fresh water; they were not used to denying themselves much; they were not used to journeys on foot." The second cause was, perhaps, yet more potent. "The affair of Big Bethel and Vienna had created a great outcry against rushing into places that people did not know anything about. I think the idea of every one was that we were to go into no such things as that—that we were to feel our way," again says McDowell. Precaution on this point was particularly emphasized in his instructions. "The three following things," says his marching order, "will not be pardonable in any commander: 1st, to come upon a battery or breastwork without a knowledge of its position; 2d, to be surprised; 3d, to fall back." Moving forward with such painful wariness, a surprise of the enemy was, of course, equally out of the question. In obedience to Beauregard's orders, his outposts everywhere retired, though, in several instances, with such precipitation as to leave their tents, knapsacks, and even their freshly cooked rations behind.

Manassas Junction lies thirty-five miles southwest of Washington, on a high, open plateau; there the rebels had some slight field-works, armed with fourteen or fifteen heavy guns, and garrisoned by about two thousand men.

Bull Run flows in a southeasterly direction, some three miles east of Manassas, with wooded heights coming generally close up to its west bank. The stream is winding and sluggish, and, though here and there it has steep, sometimes precipitous and rocky banks, it is fordable in many places. Beauregard's main army, increased now to over twenty thousand, was posted at the various fords of Bull Run, in a line some eight miles long, and extending from the Manassas Railroad to the Stone Bridge on the Warrenton turnpike.*

---

* At *Union Mills Ford*, Ewell's brigade of three regiments; at *McLean's Ford*, Jones' brigade of three regiments; at *Blackburn's Ford*, Longstreet's brigade of five regiments; above *Mitchell's Ford*, Bonham's brigade of five regiments; at *Lewis' Ford*, Cocke's brigade of portions of six regiments; at *Stone Bridge*, Evans' demi-brigade of a regiment and a half; Early's brigade of four regiments was posted as a reserve in rear and support of Longstreet and Jones. All the above, together with some seven other regiments and portions, not brigaded, constituted Beauregard's "Army of the Potomac." His official report states the total effective, on the morning of the battle (July 21st), to have been 21,833, and 29 guns.

Holmes' brigade, an independent command ordered up from Acquia Creek, consisted of two regiments, reported by Beauregard at a total of 1,355, and 6 guns. It was posted as a support for Ewell.

Johnston's "Army of the Shenandoah" consisted of Jackson's brigade of five regiments, posted as a support for Bonham; and Bee's brigade of four regiments, posted as a support for Cocke. These had arrived and were in camp on the morning of the battle (July 21st). Beauregard reports their round numbers, ready for action, at 6,000 men and 20 guns. In addition, there arrived at Manassas about noon, and on the battle-field between two and four o'clock, Fisher's Sixth North Carolina, 634, and Kirby Smith's brigade (afterward led by Elzey), of 1,700 men and 2 guns; and also Hill's Virginia Regiment, 550.

	Men.	Guns.
Recapitulation: Beauregard's army	21,833	29
Johnston's army	8,884	22
Holmes' brigade	1,355	6
	32,072	57

To which may be added sundry detachments, the numbers of which are not given in official reports.

It was McDowell's intention to turn this position on the South. To conceal his purpose, and create the impression of a contemplated attack in front, he directed his march upon Centreville on the Warrenton turnpike. On Thursday morn-

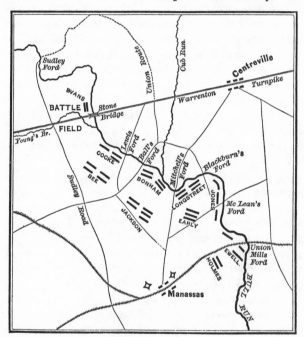

Bull Run—The Field of Strategy.

ing, July 18th, Tyler moved upon Centreville, but, arriving there at nine o'clock, he found that it, too, had been evacuated, and that Beauregard's entire army was behind Bull Run. Centreville being situated on a hill, Tyler could see the whole valley spread out before him, with Manassas on

12

the high plateau beyond. The main body of the enemy, he learned, had retired down the road running directly toward that point, crossing the stream at Mitchell's and Blackburn's fords.

Tyler's unopposed advance had perhaps inspired him and his officers with an over-confidence or undue elation; perhaps it suggested the belief that the enemy did not feel strong enough to make a stand. Under instructions to "observe well the roads," but to bring on no engagement, it occurred to him to make a reconnoissance in the direction of the retreat.

As often happens under such circumstances, the spirit of combat overcame discretion. Accompanied by Richardson, one of his brigade commanders, Tyler first went out with a squadron of cavalry and two companies of light infantry. Finding a favorable situation to try artillery, they sent back for a battery, and Richardson's brigade to support it. About noon of the 18th they were within a mile of Blackburn's ford. Then followed the ever-recurring experience of such affairs. First, an experimental cannonade from a couple of field-pieces, before which the enemy's guns retired; next the advance of a skirmish-line, before which the enemy's skirmishers retired; then an advance of some of the field-pieces and the planting of a stronger battery; the posting of a regiment to support the skirmishers, and, soon after, the posting of the entire brigade to support the regiment, followed by calling up a reserve brigade to support the first. Thus the afternoon's work drifted quickly from a reconnoissance to a skirmish, and from a skirmish to a preliminary battle. It was not until some sixty men had fallen, until the two exposed field-pieces were with difficulty extricated, until one regiment had retreated in confusion and the other three were deployed in line of battle to make a new charge, that Tyler heeded his instructions, and withdrew his reluctant officers and men from the fight, partly demoralized and generally exasperated, and returned to Centreville. In point of fact, the loss, the damage, the demoralization, had been equal on both sides. The rebel reports show that three regiments of Longstreet's brigade, which bore the first assault, were so much shaken that Early's reserve brigade of three fresh regiments was called up and relieved them, that one of these regiments was thrown into confusion, and that the rebel loss was sixty-three killed and wounded. Undecisive as it was, the battle of Blackburn's Ford had an important effect. It confirmed Beauregard in his previous impression that the principal Union attack would be made at that point on the centre of his long line. On the other hand, McDowell, receiving from his officers reports of rifle-pits and breastworks, became convinced that a direct assault was unwise. The affair of Blackburn's Ford thus proved something more than a preliminary defeat; it augmented the causes of a great disaster. Upon hearing the cannonade, McDowell had immediately ordered all the divisions forward to Centreville. He had already in his own mind given up the plan of turning the enemy's right, because of the unfavorable nature of the ground and roads. The necessity of finding an unfortified crossing seemed now also demonstrated. Meeting his division commanders at Centreville, that same night of Thursday, July 18th, McDowell informed them confidentially that he had abandoned his original plan, and had resolved to make the attack by marching northward and turning Beauregard's left flank instead of his right.

As an incident of this resolve, however, it was even more essential than before to continue to threaten the enemy's centre; and thus Richardson's brigade was once more posted in the direction of Blackburn's Ford.   Meanwhile the engineers were busy all of Friday and Saturday in efforts to find an unfortified ford over Bull Run.   They were not successful till a late hour on Saturday; and this delay deferred the main battle till Sunday, July 21st.   Could a similar attack have been made a day earlier, the result would probably have been altogether different.

CHAPTER XV.

BULL RUN.

At Centreville, on Saturday night, McDowell called his officers together and announced to them his plan of battle for the following day. The Warrenton turnpike ran almost directly west from Centreville to Gainesville station on the railroad. He was yet unaware that Johnston had joined Beauregard, and sought to prevent such junction by seizing Gainesville. Beauregard's army lay in detachments behind Bull Run, at five different fords, along a line of eight miles. His left and northernmost flank was at the stone bridge where Warrenton turnpike crosses Bull Run, though Mc-Dowell supposed it to extend to the first ford above. The bridge was a solid stone structure of two arches, of considerable size and height, connecting the precipitous and rocky eastern bank of the stream with a broad piece of level bottomland on the west. The bridge was thought to be defended in force, and said to be prepared for blowing up. The engineers had information, however, that Sudley Ford, two or three miles above, could be readily carried and crossed by an attacking column. McDowell therefore ordered that Tyler, with the heaviest division, should advance from Centreville directly to Stone Bridge, three and a half miles distant, and make a feigned attack; while Hunter and Heintzelman should make a secret and circuitous night march northward, cross Sudley Ford, and, rapidly descending on the enemy's side of Bull Run, should clear away the batteries at the stone bridge by a rear attack, and thus enable Tyler's division to cross and join in the combined march on Gainesville, or continue the attack on Beauregard's left. If the stone bridge were blown up, the engineers had timbers ready to repair it. The division of Miles should remain in reserve at Centreville, and the brigade of Richardson continue to threaten Blackburn's Ford.

In the rebel camp, the Confederate commanders were at the same time equally intent on a scheme of their own to attack and surprise McDowell. No sooner had Johnston arrived at Manassas with the second detachment of the Army of the Shenandoah, about noon of Saturday, July 20th, than Beauregard explained to him the character and course of Bull Run, and the situation of the five principal fords behind which his various brigades were posted; and since a practicable road from each of these five fords converged upon Centreville, he proposed a simultaneous advance and attack on the Union army, in its camps, early Sunday morning.

Johnston, who now as ranking officer assumed command, adopted Beauregard's plan. Part of the Army of the Shenandoah had arrived before and with him ; the remainder was expected that night. He had every reason to suppose that Patterson would promptly follow him to join McDowell. To secure the fruit of his own movement, he must therefore crush McDowell before Patterson could arrive. The orders for such an advance and attack were duly written out, and Johnston signed his approval of them in the gray twilight of Sunday morning.

An hour or two, however, revealed to him the uselessness of these orders, on which the ink was scarcely dry. At sunrise he heard Tyler's signal-guns, and soon received notice that McDowell had taken the offensive. The remainder of his Army of the Shenandoah had not arrived, as he hoped. Under these circumstances his plan of attack must be abandoned. Beauregard thereupon proposed a modification of the plan—to attack with their right from the region of Blackburn's Ford, and to stand on the defensive with their left in the neighborhood of the stone bridge. This suggestion, again, Johnston adopted and ordered to be carried out.

But the Union forces had already taken the initiative. A little past midnight McDowell's army was astir, and the three designated divisions started. Unluckily, at the very outset, Hunter and Heintzelman were delayed two or three hours by the first division not getting out of its camps in time, and failing to clear the road for them. The route proved unexpectedly long; it was nine o'clock when the advance reached Sudley Ford. The crossing, however, was not opposed, and was easily effected. From the ford the Sudley road ran south toward Manassas, crossing the Warrenton turnpike at right angles about a mile and a quarter west of the stone bridge. A little stream, called Young's Branch, also crosses both roads at this intersection, makes a circle to the northeast, and, returning, flows to the southeast into Bull Run. This was the destined battle-field.

It happened that the stone bridge was but slenderly defended. The timber had been felled to form a heavy abattis behind the bridge; but Evans, the rebel officer in charge, had only a regiment and a half, with four guns, for his entire guard. Tyler appeared in force before the bridge, and began his demonstration; but made it so feebly that Evans soon became convinced no real assault was intended; and having learned the actual crossing at Sudley Ford, he at about nine o'clock withdrew all but four companies and two guns from the bridge, and hastened to the rear to throw himself across Hunter's path. The Union approach having become plainly discernible, Evans posted his eleven companies on the ridge immediately north of the Warrenton turnpike and Young's Branch, his left resting on the Sudley road, with one gun at his left, and the other some dis-

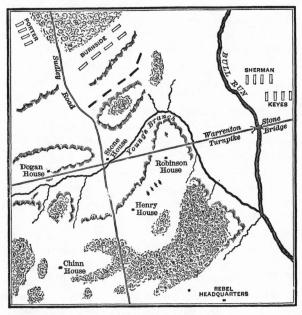

Bull Run—Battle of the Forenoon.*

tance behind his right, on the point of a hill south of Young's Branch.

---

* In these maps the topographical features are copied from the accurate official maps published by the Engineer Bureau of the War Department. The position of the troops is of course only conjectural, but based on the descriptions and inferences in the official reports of both armies.

At ten o'clock Hunter's advance emerged from the woods into open fields, about a mile north of the Warrenton turnpike, the scattering shots of the skirmishers having already opened the conflict. On both sides everything was raw and awkward—officers and men, staff and line. There was undue excitement and impetuosity, mixed with unnecessary confusion and delay. None of the reports specify how the battle began; the mere momentum of the march seems to have carried the advance regiments under the first shower of rebel shells and bullets at distances varying from five hundred to one thousand yards. A preliminary artillery duel sprang up, under which Burnside led his four regiments after his battery into the fields to the left of the Sudley road. With a little more deliberation and a united onset, these would easily have brushed away Evans' thin line; but, in the delay incident to the first actual experiment of battle, the rebels gained opportunity to bring up substantial reinforcements. Four regiments and two companies of Johnston's Army of the Shenandoah, under General Bee, hurried up and formed to the right and a little in advance of Evans' original line, while Imboden's battery of four guns took position on a hill in the rear, south of the Warrenton turnpike. Thus disposed, with little disparity in strength between attack and defence, the first stubborn contest of the day appears to have taken place, lasting perhaps from eleven o'clock till noon. The Union troops pressed forward with determined courage; the rebels resisted with such spirit that Burnside became apprehensive for his Rhode Island battery, and Sykes' battalion of regulars was sent to strengthen his left. By this time Hunter had sent Porter's brigade into the fields to the right of the Sudley road, where Griffin's battery could engage the rebel field-pieces; Heintzelman was hurrying up with an advance regiment and

Ricketts' battery. Under this combined pressure the Confederate line wavered, yielded, and finally broke. Their left retreated stubbornly down the hill, and, rallying again, endeavored to make a stand behind a stone house at the intersection of the two roads; but a vigorous Union charge down the Sudley road completed their dispersion. The whole first formation of the enemy was swept southward more than half a mile, entirely across and out of the valley of Young's Branch. But the advantage was not won without considerable damage to the Union troops, the demoralization of several regiments, and the serious loss of valuable officers. General Hunter himself was wounded by a shell at the very beginning of the action, compelling his retirement from the front, and devolving the command of his division on Porter.

McDowell, who came upon the field by way of Sudley Ford as the battle began, had already sent back word to Tyler to press his attack at the stone bridge. Such an attack, however, was now no longer necessary. We have seen how Evans had withdrawn to oppose Hunter; and the four companies he left behind had also retired southward. Avoiding the bridge with its *abattis*, Tyler led Sherman's and Keyes' brigades across Bull Run half a mile above, where the stream was fordable for infantry, and, marching over a mile of level bottom-land, so directed their course by the firing that they effected a safe junction with Hunter's division, Keyes remaining on the extreme left. They approached the morning's battle-field from the northeast; Sherman reported to McDowell, and joined the general pursuit, directing his march to the right. Keyes remained on the left, and under Tyler's personal orders; and thus it turned out that this single brigade became and remained an independent detachment during the whole day, separated by a wide interval from the main battle in the afternoon, and not being in a position to receive orders from McDowell.

It has been explained that the first rebel line was composed mainly of Johnston's troops. As they retreated up the hill south of Young's Branch, Jackson's brigade of five regiments, also of Johnston's army, was just arriving there on its way to guard the stone bridge, and only at that moment learning the true state of affairs. This hill south of Young's Branch was a higher and stronger position than that from which Evans and Bee had been driven. Its crest ran in a westerly curve from the Robinson house, near the Warrenton turnpike, past the Henry house near the Sudley road, both being within the southeastern angle of the intersection. The two roads cross in the valley at Young's Branch, and from their crossing ascend gently to the east, west, north, and south.

On this crest, Jackson, with the ready instinct of combat, formed a new line. His five regiments and two batteries, stretched from the Robinson to the Henry houses, formed a solid-looking protection, behind which some of the flying rebels gathered courage and rallied in little driblets. Bee's five regiments had shrunk to about four companies, and the remaining fugitives were moving in hopeless panic down the Sudley road toward Manassas, spreading direful tidings of disaster. Jackson's line was rendered yet stronger by having Hampton's battalion—that morning arrived from Richmond—on its extreme right in the turnpike before the Robinson house; and behind these, Bee's fragments were gathered into a sheltering ravine.

At this period of the day, a little after noon, the advancing Union columns had their best co-operation and strongest momentum. Keyes' brigade was advancing on the left toward the Robinson hill. Sherman was moving diagonally across the centre of the morning's field. Porter's still aggressive brigade was pushing down the Sudley road.

The compact brigades of Franklin and Willcox were coming to the front on the right. Moreover, Griffin's and Ricketts' batteries had obtained favorable positions near the Dogan house, with an enfilading fire against Hampton. Toward two o'clock two regiments of Keyes' brigade made a charge up the Robinson hill and drove Hampton out of the tangle of fences and hedges about the Robinson House, though newly planted rebel batteries farther to the rear made it impossible to hold the position. The whole Union line swung forward to the Warrenton turnpike; and while the rebel reports pass it over with the merest allusions, it seems probable that, like Hampton, other portions of Jackson's line were moved somewhat farther back, to find better shelter from the annoying fire of the Union batteries. This mid-day Union success seemed, and was, sweeping and complete; but it proved seriously deceptive in the further operations of the afternoon, which it naturally suggested and provoked.

A little before this time the Confederate commanders woke up to the true nature of the conflict. Beauregard was yet waiting impatiently to hear that his right was advancing on Centreville, when, toward eleven o'clock, word came that, through a miscarriage of orders, that enterprise was just being commenced. Realizing now that McDowell's attack was not a mere feint, they countermanded the Centreville movement, ordered all available reserves forward to the main battle, and themselves hurriedly galloped to the front. Here they now put their personal exertions, encouragement, and example, into the somewhat unpromising task of miti-gating a disastrous defeat, rather than with even remote hope of turning the scale to victory.

The Confederates had been literally driven into the woods, the edge of which formed a sort of semicircle on the second ridge south of Warrenton turnpike and east of the Sudley road. But this reverse brought certain important advantages. Their retreat not only concentrated their regiments ; it also, for the first time during the day, concentrated their artillery, thirteen pieces of which were posted near together to the centre and right, so as to give a partial cross-fire at

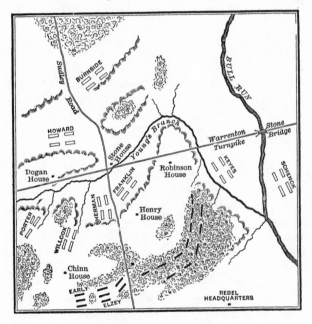

Bull Run—Battle of the Afternoon.

a distance of three hundred to six hundred yards over the whole open plateau or hill about the Henry house and toward the Robinson house. Under the personal directions of Johnston and Beauregard, they now formed their line along this semicircular edge of woods, with the advantage of a fringe of second-growth pines in their front to afford them almost perfect concealment. Their right extended to where the hill descends to Young's Branch; their left reached nearly to the Sudley road. It is needless to specify the several corps in detail; the nearest reinforcements were already arriving; Johnston's report sums up the strength of this completed line at twelve regiments, twenty-two guns, and two companies of cavalry. The formation well begun, Beauregard took personal command, while Johnston, as chief, returned to the rebel headquarters to keep his eye on the entire field.

Reduced by losses, McDowell's numbers were now little, if any, superior to the enemy; for the brigade of Keyes was separated from him, working its way southward along Young's Branch in the hope to make a flank attack on the rebel right; in reality it rendered no further substantial help. Howard's brigade, held back as a reserve, was not yet at hand. McDowell's effective force consisted of the brigades of Porter, Franklin, Willcox, and Sherman, a total of fourteen regiments, but several of which were already seriously demoralized; these were massed in sheltered situations in the valley along the turnpike and Young's Branch, mainly west of the intersection of the roads. All the advantages of position during the day had been with McDowell; now they were suddenly turned against him by the very success he had gained. The enemy was on the height, he at the foot of the hill. The enemy needed only to defend a stationary line; he must move forward under a prepared fire. They were concealed in chosen positions; he must mount into open view. They could repel in combination; he must risk successive assaults. His men had been under arms since midnight—most of them had made a march of ten miles through the sweltering July heat. They were flushed with victory, but also lulled thereby into the false security of thinking their work accomplished, when in reality its sternest effort was merely about to begin.

The situation naturally dictated an attack on the rebel centre and left flank, and, had this been unitedly and solidly made, it must unquestionably have succeeded even against the disadvantage already mentioned. But right here the want of proper staff organization and discipline, and the rawness of the troops in manœuvre, proved a fatal defect; and the severe conflict of the next hour and a half resolved itself into a somewhat spasmodic and intermittent struggle on both sides.

When, at about half-past two o'clock, the batteries of Ricketts and Griffin were ordered to move forward from the Dogan heights across the valley to the top of the Henry hill, they did so with the feeling that the two regiments ordered to follow and support them were tardy, inadequate, and unreliable. Other regiments, moving forward to the flank attack, could not well be observed, because of the uneven ground and the intervening woods and bushes. The rebels had disappeared; there was a complete lull in the battle. But danger was no less at hand. Hardly had Ricketts taken his post before his cannoneers and horses began to fall under the accurate fire of near and well-concealed rebel sharpshooters. Death puffed from bushes, fences, buildings; and yet the jets of flame and wreaths of smoke were the only visible enemy to assail. Officers and cannoneers held on with a desperate courage; some moved to new positions to foil the rebel range. Griffin's battery came and took place alongside; eleven Union guns and thirteen Confederate guns were confronted at short range in a stubborn and exciting duel. But now the rebel regiments, seeing the dangerous exposure of the Union batteries, were tempted to swarm out of their cover. They pressed cautiously but tenaciously upon Ricketts. Griffin, absorbed in directing the fire of two of his guns against the rebel batteries, was suddenly startled at seeing a regiment advancing boldly on his right, in open view. Their very audacity puzzled him. They could hardly be friends, he thought; yet was it possible that foes were so near and would take such a risk? Instinctively he ordered his guns to be charged with canister and trained upon them. Yet at the dreadful thought of pouring such a volley upon a Union regiment, he once more hesitated, and held a brief colloquy with Major Barry, chief of artillery. "Captain," said Barry, "they are your battery support." "They are Confederates," replied Griffin, in intense excitement; "as certain as the world, they are Confederates." "No," answered Barry; "I know they are your battery support." Griffin spurred forward, and told his officer not to fire. The mistake proved fatal. During this interval of doubt the Confederate regiment had approached to point-blank range, and levelled their muskets just as Griffin gave his order to desist. Griffin's canister would have annihilated the regiment; but now the tables were turned, and in an instant the regiment's volley had annihilated Griffin's and Ricketts' batteries. Officers and men fell smitten with death and wounds, and horses and caissons went tearing in wild disorder down the hill, breaking and scattering the ascending line of battle. Under this sudden catastrophe the supporting regiment stood a while spellbound with mingled astonishment and terror. They were urged forward to repel the advance on the guns; but the unexpected disaster overawed them; under the continued and still advancing volleys of the same rebel regiment, they fired their muskets, turned, and fled.

These disabled batteries, visible to both armies, now became the centre and coveted prize of an irregular contest, which surged back and forth over the plateau of the Henry hill; but, whether because of confusion of orders, or the broken surface of the ground, or more probably the mere reciprocal eagerness of capture and rescue, the contest was carried on, not by the whole line, but by single regiments, or at most by two or three regiments moving accidentally rather than designedly in concert. Several times the fight raged past and over the prostrate body of Ricketts, lying wounded among his guns, and who was finally carried away a prisoner to Richmond. The rebels would dash forward, capture the batteries, and endeavor to turn the pieces on the Union lines; then a Union regiment would sweep up the hill, drive them back, and essay to drag the guns down into safe possession. And a similar shifting and intermitting fight went on, not merely on this single spot, but also among the low concealing pines of the middle ground in front, as well as in the oak-woods on the Union right, where at times friend became intermingled with foe, and where both sides took occasional prisoners near the same place.

In this prolonged and wasteful struggle the Union strength was slowly and steadily consumed. Arnold's battery crossed the valley to the support of Griffin and Ricketts, but found itself obliged to again withdraw. The Rhode Island battery took part in the contest as well as it might from the hill north of Young's Branch. Brigade after brigade—Sherman's, Franklin's, Willcox's, and finally Howard's reserve, were brought forward—regiment after regiment was sent up the hill—three times the batteries were recovered and again lost. It speaks volumes for the courage of the raw, undisciplined volunteers, that, in the face of these repeated failures, they continued to go perseveringly against what seemed to them a hidden and unattainable barrier, until a stronger wave of rebel bullets or bayonets, surging suddenly

I.—9

forward in the pine thicket, would meet and force them back.

In the endeavor to outflank and envelop the rebel left, the Union right had become so strongly turned southward that it was nearly parallel to the Sudley road.   Near the beginning of this final contest, Johnston received notice that the long-expected remainder of his Army of the Shenandoah had at length come ; and before it was half over, Elzey, with Kirby Smith's brigade of three regiments, arrived near the battle-field from Manassas by the Sudley road.   By this time, too, four other regiments, two from Cocke's and two from Bonham's brigades, also came up from the nearer fords.   These seven fresh regiments, thrown opportunely by the rebel commander into the woods west of the Sudley road, directly against the exposed Union right flank, created a numerical overweight, which affords sufficient explanation of the Union repulse at that point.

But now, at half-past four in the afternoon, when the Union reinforcements were exhausted, the rebel accessions still continued : Early with three regiments arrived from the lower fords ; Holmes with two regiments, and Ewell with three others, were rapidly approaching.   Before the arrival of these last the battle was already decided.   Early's brigade was sent cautiously through the woods, still farther to the rebel left, and suddenly appeared with Beckham's battery on the heights near the Chinn house, three-quarters of a mile west of the Sudley road, and entirely beyond and in the rear of the Union right.

The Union troops, having approached the second stage of the battle in such a flush of success, and with such an apparent assurance of victory, could not for a time realize the stern fact that the contest was turning against them.   Officers of experience and sagacity, indeed, became seriously alarmed for the final result, when Griffin's and Ricketts' batteries were destroyed; but for the greater part it was looked upon as an untoward accident, and operated rather to inspire the already related efforts for their recovery. The feeling of course gradually changed with the successive failures to gain and permanently hold the hill. As brigade after brigade melted away in the repeated efforts, even the men in the ranks could not omit to note the rapid diminution of the available strength. Some of the repulsed regiments kept their organization and returned heroically to the charge. Others, on the contrary, not having that slowly acquired force of discipline which makes cohesion a second nature of the soldier and creates an instinctive reliance on mutual support as the surest means of safety, considered their duty done with a single charge, and, once driven back, went to pieces like the adjournment of a mass meeting. In this shortcoming, officers were as culpable as the men, for war combines art with science, and the superior work of the veteran comes through long years of practice. It must be remembered that these were only three months volunteers, and besides, as such, the most impulsive and independent men in their several communities, whose innate promptness of thought and action had brought them to the very forefront of the civil war. Lacking long drill and discipline, they acted upon individual judgment and impulse, rather than as organized bodies merely executing the orders of their officers. This explains to us the remarkable statement of Captain Woodbury, that, "at four o'clock, on the 21st, there were more than twelve thousand volunteers on the battle-field of Bull Run who had entirely lost their regimental organization. They could no longer be handled as troops, for the officers and men were not together. Men and officers mingled together promiscuously; and it is worthy of remark that this disorganization did not result from defeat or fear." One other fact must be remembered in extenuation: that with the long night march, the burning heat of the day, and the new and intense excitements of the battle-field, the men, famished with hunger and thirst, were becoming physically exhausted.

When, therefore, at half-past four o'clock, the two fresh Confederate brigades had repulsed the Union flank attack west of the Sudley road, and Early's rebel brigade with Beckham's battery suddenly burst through the woods near the Chinn house, still farther to the west, with a vigorous and startling attack on the Union flank and rear, throwing into quick confusion and retreat a detachment of Union cavalry stationed in apparent retirement and safety, the battle came to a speedy termination by a sort of universal consent; a realization and acknowledgment of coming defeat pervaded the whole army, and found instant expression in increased disorganization and immediate movement toward a general retreat. Whatever may have been the other discouragements, the main impulse of this movement came from the universal belief that Johnston's army had now arrived, and that success had thereby become hopeless. The question of Johnston's possible presence in the battle had run through the Centreville camps, and there were rumors of his coming on Saturday night; but the army apparently had no suspicion that it was fighting him all day Sunday, till the moment of the attack on the extreme left by one of Beauregard's brigades. That attack from an unexpected quarter seemed convincing proof of the presence of a new and additional force, and therefore roused the quick instinct of retreat, not so much in acknowledgment of actual defeat, as in prudent avoidance of irresistible slaughter or capture by overwhelming numbers.

CHAPTER XVI.

THE RETREAT.

, THE suddenness of their victory was entirely unexpected by the rebels. Signs of disaster to themselves were as strong as to the Federals to the very last. Intense curiosity and solicitude had brought Jefferson Davis from Richmond. It is related that, as he was riding to the battle-field from Manassas, at about four o'clock that afternoon, he met such a stream of panic-stricken rebel soldiers, and heard such direful tidings from the front, that his companions were thoroughly convinced the Confederates had lost the day, and implored him to turn back for personal safety. He went on, against their advice, to find that the conflict was already over, and to learn, with mingled amazement and joy, that the Union army had, by a sudden and unexplained impulse, ceased fighting, and half marched, half run from the field.

McDowell was no less astounded at his own overwhelming reverse. A little before Elzey and Early appeared on his right to outflank him, there had been a lull in the Confederate firing that led him to hope the enemy was giving way. At the very worst there seemed no doubt of his ability to hold the Warrenton turnpike and stone bridge and maintain free communication with Centreville. For this abundant resources were yet available. Burnside's brigade had remained in reserve on the morning's battle-field, and, after four hours' rest, was yet capable of effective service. Keyes' brigade beyond the hill, on his left, was substantially unharmed. Schenck had an almost fresh brigade at the stone bridge. Miles had a brigade at Centreville, which could be replaced from Runyon's division near Vienna. The engineers had cleared away the *abattis* at the stone bridge. The hills north of the Warrenton turnpike were excellent defensive positions. It needed but *morale* among the troops to hold the battle-ground, and holding this would have compelled the enemy to retreat.

Unfortunately the Union army had lost its *morale*. The mere disorder of the final repulse was slight; but the demoralization and loss of discipline had been growing during the whole afternoon, until, of a sudden, the army was half-dissolved. The impulse of retreat once started, there was no checking or controlling it. Despite the efforts and appeals of McDowell and his officers, the various detachments began moving from the field. The commander yielded to necessity, made the best dispositions he could to cover the retreat, and passed the word to reassemble in the old camps at Centreville, not doubting that he could there make a rally.

The way thither by the Warrenton turnpike was open and straight; the distance four and a half miles. But, through the perversity of fate, each detachment now retreated by the same road over which it had come. Thus the bulk of the army—the brigades of Porter, Burnside, Franklin, Willcox, and Howard—went back over the long detour of ten miles round by Sudley Ford; these had with them, as yet, two batteries—a total of ten field-pieces; for only the batteries of Ricketts and Griffin were lost in the main battle. Sherman's brigade, on the other hand, marched eastward, over the ground of the morning's conflict, and recrossed Bull

Run at the ford, half a mile above the stone bridge, by which they had approached. Keyes' brigade, becoming aware of the general retreat, also returned by that route. These two, with Schenck's brigade, soon reached the Warrenton road, making a comparatively easy march to Centreville.

It also becomes necessary to mention here that, while the main battle of the afternoon was going on, a second engagement had been fought at Blackburn's Ford. The brigades of Richardson and of Davies were sent there in the morning, to make such demonstrations as would mask McDowell's real movement. In the afternoon, however, their purpose became apparent; and to relieve the stress of the main battle, the Confederate commander sent orders to Jones' brigade to cross Bull Run and make a demonstration. At about four o'clock, Jones, with his three regiments, crossed at McLean's Ford, and endeavored, by a flank movement, to capture Hunt's battery stationed with Davies' brigade. Davies quietly watched the oncoming rebel regiments, rearranged his lines, and held his fire in reserve till the enemy were deploying to form line of battle. They had advanced within five hundred yards, only, however, to find themselves embarrassed by woods and broken ground. In this situation and dilemma Davies ordered Hunt's battery of six guns to open upon them with grape and canister. The rebel official report characterizes it as a "murderous shower," and, no doubt, correctly. It scattered the attacking column as if by enchantment; in thirty minutes there was not a soldier of them to be seen, and Jones modestly reports a loss in the affair of fourteen killed and sixty-two wounded.

It was now near sundown. Miles, commanding at Centreville, either through illness or drunkenness, had become incapable of duty—a situation whose serious consequences were averted by the prudence and good behavior of the three brigade commanders. But, from this cause, premature orders were received by the two brigades of Davies and Richardson to fall back on Centreville; while to Blenker the more judicious order was given to advance his brigade toward Stone Bridge, which he did, deploying it in line of battle across the Warrenton turnpike, half-way between Centreville and Cub Run.

As soon as Johnston and Beauregard had sufficiently recovered from their astonishment at seeing the Union army in unmistakable retreat, they ordered pursuit to be made, but, as it would seem, with the greatest caution. In truth, McDowell's vanquished brigades marched from the immediate battle-field only half-disbanded; there remained, in most instances, a little nucleus at least of each organization, which yet, for a time, held together, while several of the brigades were nearly intact. Thus it happened that, while the battalion of rebel cavalry under Stuart was ordered to pursue along the Sudley road, they found the Union forces generally so compact, and the rear so well protected, that they could only dash in here and there and pick up or scatter isolated squads of stragglers. Another reserve battalion of rebel cavalry under Radford was sent in pursuit from the vicinity of Ball's Ford up toward the turnpike; while Johnston also sent orders to Bonham to take the remainder of his own and Longstreet's brigades, and move against the line of retreat at Centreville. Radford, like Stuart, saw that the retreating brigades of Sherman, Keyes, and Schenck were too formidable to attack; and Bonham, on nearing Centreville, found the brigades of Blenker, Richardson, and Davies so well posted, and so superior in numbers, that he was quite content to stop with a mere reconnoissance, and at nightfall returned to his camps behind Mitchell's and Blackburn's

Fords. Meanwhile, though the Confederate pursuit could nowhere venture a serious assault, an accident served to greatly enlarge their harvest of trophies.

The business of war was such a novelty, that McDowell's army accumulated an extraordinary number of camp-followers and non-combatants. The vigilant newspapers of the chief cities sent a cloud of correspondents to chronicle the incidents of the march and conflict. The volunteer regiments carried with them personal sympathies and companionships unknown to regular armies. Congress had met in special session; and senators and representatives, full of the patriotic hope and pride of their several States, no less than their own eager political solicitude, in several instances joined in what many rashly assumed would be a mere triumphal parade. McDowell's unopposed and apparently irresistible advance through the enemy's outposts lured them on to Centreville in a false security; and the uniformly favorable reports which went back to Washington even brought out a fresh accession of the same material on Sunday morning of the battle.

By that time, however, the situation had become more serious, and generally made the non-combatants somewhat circumspect. Only a few of hardier courage followed to the battle-field; most of them remained at Centreville until the cannonade announced the beginning of the fight, and then drifted gradually down the turnpike toward the stone bridge, not nearer than a mile and a half to the actual fighting, but where they could hear the volleys, see the smoke and dust, and perhaps the occasional manœuvres of Schenck's and Keyes' brigades. In a certain sense they were under fire, because the long-range shells of the field-pieces rendered even that locality somewhat dangerous. From this situation were written many highly sensational, but purely

imaginary and most grotesquely confused accounts of the
battle, first published in the newspapers. A famous corre-
spondent of the *London Times*, who earned the sobriquet of
"Bull Run Russell," wrote his description of the affair for
European readers, after a leisurely lunch at Centreville, and
a stroll of perhaps a mile toward Stone Bridge, taking his
departure with the earliest fugitives.

It also happened that on the afternoon of the battle a
considerable number of provision, baggage, and ammunition wagons, together with some private vehicles of the
non-combatants heretofore mentioned, had been sent down
the Warrenton turnpike from Centreville, toward the stone
bridge. When finally the first wave of fugitives brought
unfavorable news from the front, these began a general
movement in return, which unavoidably produced quick
confusion and blockade; and it was chiefly among these
that the disgraceful panic and flight, which has furnished
the nearly universal theme of criticism of the battle, first
broke out. Naturally the tide of disaster rose quick and
high; the retreating brigades, and nearer approach of cannonade and musketry, soon confirmed the worst fears of
overwhelming defeat and pressing pursuit, and started a
veritable scramble and stampede for safety. Arms and
clothing were thrown away by those on foot; wagons were
abandoned, and even ambulances with wounded soldiers
left standing in the road, while the frightened teamsters
rode away at headlong speed, on horses unhitched or cut
out of their harness.

It would seem that things had already come to this pass
before the columns which were retreating around the long
detour by way of Sudley Springs and Ford once more came
in sight of the Warrenton turnpike, at a point between
Stone Bridge and Cub Run. Cub Run seems to have been

a difficult little stream, provided with a "suspension bridge" of some kind where the turnpike crosses it. Radford's cavalry had not only been hovering along and occasionally dashing in on the turnpike, but a rebel light battery succeeded in establishing itself where it commanded the "suspension bridge." When the retreating column from Sudley Ford came in sight, they found to their consternation that it was necessary to run the gauntlet of this artillery fire. "The enemy opened fire," says Burnside's report, "upon the retreating mass of men. Upon the bridge crossing Cub Run, a shot took effect upon the horses of a team that was crossing. The wagon was overturned directly in the centre of the bridge, and the passage was completely obstructed. The enemy continued to play his artillery upon the train, carriages, ambulances, and artillery wagons that filled up the road, and these were reduced to ruin. The artillery could not possibly pass, and five pieces of the Rhode Island battery, which had been safely brought off the field, were here lost." The four pieces of Arnold's battery were also abandoned here from this cause. Four pieces of Carlisle's battery were apparently lost in the same neighborhood, though from a charge of Radford's cavalry. This "suspension bridge" over Cub Run was distant some three miles from the main battle-field, and it was here that the enemy made his largest capture of guns and wagons.

It may be imagined that at Confederate headquarters that night the measure of satisfaction was well-nigh full. Yet that their rejoicing was tempered with a serious alloy of rebel danger and losses, is also clearly enough revealed in Jefferson Davis' telegraphic bulletins. "A terrible battle is raging," said his first. "We have won a glorious, though dear-bought victory," was the language of his second. In his third he repeated, "Night has closed upon a hard-fought field. Our forces have won a glorious victory." He forbore to add, what the official reports and correspondence afterward developed, namely: that not only was the field "hard-fought" and the victory "dear-bought," but they were by no means confident it was final. On the contrary, the rebel headquarters was in serious apprehension lest McDowell should turn from Centreville and once more assail the Confederate right flank at or below Blackburn's Ford. To meet this reported danger, Ewell and Holmes were that night ordered post-haste back to Union Mills. "You will not fail to remember," afterward wrote Jefferson Davis to Beauregard, "that, so far from knowing the enemy was routed, a large part of our forces was moved by you, in the night of the 21st, to repel a supposed attack upon our right, and the next day's operations did not fully reveal what has since been reported of the enemy's panic."

When McDowell left the battle-field his intention and orders were to rally at Centreville. But, arriving there, he found the conditions less favorable than he anticipated. It had been designed that Blenker's brigade should, during the day, throw up intrenchments ; this was not done, because the necessary tools did not get forward as expected. Next he found that Davies and Richardson had left their stations at Blackburn's Ford and were falling back. "Great God! Richardson," exclaimed McDowell, on meeting that officer, "why didn't you hold on to the position at Blackburn's Ford?" "Colonel Miles ordered me to retreat to Centreville, and I obeyed the order ; Colonel Miles is continually interfering with me, and he is drunk, and is not fit to command," was the reply. The officer stood justified, for Mc-Dowell had already suspended Miles from command. The retrograde movement was stopped, the brigades were faced about and put in the best possible line of defence, with orders to hold the position. Repairing again to Centreville, McDowell found still further discouragement in the loss of the thirteen guns at Cub Run and the increased disorder among the troops. When, toward nine o'clock—just about night-fall for that season—the last brigade reached Centreville, and the various commanders were called together, it was generally agreed that it was unwise to undertake to make a stand, as contemplated. "The condition of our artillery and its ammunition," says McDowell's report, "and the want of food for the men, who had generally abandoned or thrown away all that had been issued the day before, and the utter disorganization and consequent demoralization of the mass of the army, seemed to all who were near enough to be consulted—division and brigade commanders and staff—to admit of no alternative but to fall back." If these reasons might be questioned, there was still another absolutely conclusive. The enlistment of the three months men was expiring. The Pennsylvania Fourth, which had insisted upon and received its discharge that very morning, while the army was advancing to battle, " moved to the rear to the sound of the enemy's cannon." " In the next few days," continues McDowell, " day by day I should have lost ten thousand of the best armed, drilled, officered, and disciplined troops in the army." The practical logic of war is stern and swift. Even while the officers were deliberating, the disorganized fugitives, in a contagious and increasing panic, were already on the march. Toward ten o'clock McDowell began to distribute his orders to retire from Centreville; and a little after midnight Richardson's and Blenker's brigades marched away from that village in a deliberate and orderly retreat, maintaining their organization as a steady and effective rear-guard till they once more reached the Potomac camps.

CHAPTER XVII.

CONCLUSION.

THE official reports show a loss to the Union side in the battle of Bull Run of 25 guns (the Confederates claim 28), 481 men killed, 1,011 men wounded, and 1,460 wounded and other Union soldiers sent as prisoners to Richmond. On the Confederate side the loss was 387 killed, 1,582 wounded, and a few prisoners taken.

These simple figures prove the engagement to have been well contested and fought with equal courage and persistence by both sides. Greatly ridiculed and denounced when it occurred, the battle of Bull Run is gradually finding its vindication. General Sherman says it was " one of the best-planned battles of the war, but one of the worst-fought," and that "both armies were fairly defeated." General Johnston says : " If the tactics of the Federals had been equal to their strategy, we should have been beaten." To the military student, Bull Run, with its extended field of strategy, its quick changes of plan, its fluctuating chances and combinations, and its rapidly shifting incidents and accidents, is a most interesting, and likely to become a typical, " game of war " between volunteer armies.

The loyal people in Washington were rejoicing over a victory, steadily reported during the greater part of the day, when suddenly, at about five o'clock, came the startling telegram : " General McDowell's army in full retreat through Centreville. The day is lost. Save Washington and the remnants of this army." General Scott refused to credit the astounding and unwelcome intelligence. Nevertheless he put the Alexandria and Arlington camps into activity, sent confidential notice to Baltimore, called reinforcements from Harrisburg and New York, and suggested to McClellan to " come down to the Shenandoah Valley with such troops as can be spared from Western Virginia." By midnight, officers and civilians who were lucky enough to have retained horses began to arrive, and the apparent proportions of the defeat to increase. It was a gloomy night, but yet gloomier days followed. Next day, Monday, the rain commenced falling in torrents, and continued for thirty-six hours with but slight intermission. Through this rain the disbanded soldiers began to pour into Washington City, fagged out, hungry, and dejected, and having literally nowhere to turn their feet or lay their head. History owes a page of honorable mention to the Federal capital for its unselfish generosity on this occasion. The rich and poor, the high and low of her loyal people, with one quick and entirely unprompted impulse opened their doors and dealt out food and refreshment to the footsore, haggard, and half-starved men, whom ill-luck rather than their own delinquency had so unexpectedly reduced to tramps and fugitives.

The evil was, however, quickly remedied. By Monday noon the full extent of the disaster, though not yet certainly known, could be reasonably estimated, since indications began to show that the enemy had not pressed their pursuit in force. But, in due preparation for the worst, and in addition to all possible precautions for local defence, General McClellan was called to Washington to take command, McDowell being continued in charge of the defenses on the

Virginia side of the Potomac. Patterson's time having expired, he was mustered out of the service ; Banks was sent
to Harper's Ferry, Dix put in command at Baltimore, and
Rosecrans in West Virginia.

Coming to Washington under the favorable acquaintance-
ship and estimate of General Scott, and with the prestige of
his recent success in West Virginia, McClellan's arrival was
hailed by officials and citizens with something more than
ordinary warmth and satisfaction. This good opinion was
greatly augmented by the General's own personal conduct.
He exhibited at once a promising energy and industry in
repairing the shattered army organization ; cleared Washington City of stragglers ; established a more perfect military
discipline than had hitherto been maintained ; displayed
great tact in his first intercourse with both junior and senior
officers ; was free, affable, kind, patient, and attentive to all ;
manifested great talent and unceasing watchfulness in the
details of military administration ; and being young, vigilant, cheerful, intelligent, and apparently possessed of great
professional skill, he reaped, almost at a single harvest, a
well-nigh universal popularity.

It is in its political aspects that Bull Run becomes a great
historical landmark. To say that the hope and enthusiasm
of the North received a painful shock of humiliation and
disappointment, is to use but a mild description of the popular feeling. This first experience of defeat—or recognition
of even the possibility of defeat—was inexpressibly bitter.
Stifling the sharp sorrow, however, the great public of the
Free States sent up its prompt and united demand that the
contest should be continued and the disgrace wiped out.
Impatience and over eagerness were chastened and repressed ;
and the North reconciled itself to the painful prospect of a
tedious civil war all the more readily because of the necessity

of bending every energy to immediate preparation on a widely extended scale.

If the North was cast down by the result of Bull Run, the South was in even a greater ratio encouraged and strengthened. Vanity of personal prowess is a weakness of Southern character; and Bull Run became to the unthinking a demonstration of Southern invincibility. To the more cautious leaders the event was yet sufficiently flattering to inspire them with full confidence in ultimate success. Perhaps the most potent influence of the battle was upon foreign nations, who now looked upon the Confederate States as a belligerent of " great expectations ; " while speculative foreign capital turned somewhat eagerly to this promising new field of contraband trade.

An important event, so silent in its operation that the public was scarcely conscious it was occurring, now became the pivot and controlling force of military operations. This was the disbandment of the three months volunteers. Within a few weeks almost the whole seventy-five thousand men were mustered out and returned to their homes. Only a few regiments re-enlisted with organizations even approximately unbroken ; but out of the whole number of troops thus suddenly dissolved a considerable proportion immediately entered the three years service as individuals, and in many instances their drill and experience secured them election or appointment as officers in the new regiments. Thus the disappearance of an army brought a certain compensation ; it not only furnished the new volunteers a quickening leaven, but that portion which went home to every Free State, and to some of the Border Slave States, served to greatly strengthen and correct public opinion in their several localities.

The three years quota, and the increase of the regular

14

army, called by President Lincoln in advance of strict authority of law at the beginning of May, had so far progressed that garrisons and camps suffered no serious diminution. Congress, being convened in special session, now legalized their enlistment, perfected their organization, and made liberal provision for their equipment and supply. It authorized an army of five hundred thousand men, and a national loan of two hundred and fifty millions of dollars; it provided an increase of the navy to render the blockade vigilant and rigorous; and enforcement, revenue, confiscation, and piracy laws were enacted or amended to meet the exigencies of active rebellion.

Pending the change and transformation of the volunteer forces from the three months to the three years service, military operations necessarily came to a general cessation. Washington City, especially, and the fortified strip of territory held by the Union armies on the Virginia side of the Potomac, once more became a great military camp. Here, under McClellan's personal supervision, grew up that famous Army of the Potomac, about which future volumes of this series will have much to say. But in its formation, organization, complete equipment, and thorough drill the second half of the year 1861 passed away. A few intensely exciting incidents occurred, of which the Ball's Bluff disaster was, perhaps, the chief; but their consideration in detail does not fall within the scope of the present volume.

In the rebel camps, also, inaction was both a policy and a necessity during the remainder of the year. The trophies of Bull Run having been gathered up, and its glory vaunted in Southern newspapers and stump speeches, the rebel commander once more advanced his outposts to the positions held before the battle, while the bulk of his army turned Manassas into a fortified camp. Some of the earliest reasons for this course are explained by Johnston with blunt frankness. "The Confederate army," he writes, "was more disorganized by victory than that of the United States by defeat. The Southern volunteers believed that the objects of the war had been accomplished by their victory, and that they had achieved all that their country required of them. Many, therefore, in ignorance of their military obligations, left the army, not to return. Some hastened home to exhibit the trophies picked up on the field; others left their regiments without ceremony to attend to wounded friends, frequently accompanying them to hospitals in distant towns. Such were the reports of general and staff officers and railroad officials. Exaggerated ideas of victory prevailing among our troops cost us more men than the Federal army lost by defeat."

It would appear that, about a month after the battle of Bull Run, the rebel commanders invited Jefferson Davis to Manassas to discuss a plan of active operations for the autumn. Generals Johnston, Beauregard, and G. W. Smith proposed "the concentration there of all the available forces of the Confederate States, crossing the Potomac into Maryland at the nearest ford with this army, and placing it in rear of Washington. This," writes Johnston, "we thought would compel McClellan to fight with the chances of battle against him. Success would bring Maryland into the Confederacy, we thought, and enable us to transfer the war to the northern border of that State, where the defensive should be resumed." Davis' conclusive reply was, "that the whole country was applying for arms and troops; that he could take none from other points for that army."

Of the larger aspects of the civil war during the fall and winter of 1861, this volume does not afford further room to give even a summary. Starting with a series of favorable accidents in the spring, the rebellion had confidently expected to hold every slave-holding State. So far from realizing this hope, the end of the year witnessed the substantial loss to the conspiracy of the four important Border States of Maryland, West Virginia, Kentucky, and Missouri. This, together with the effective blockade instituted on the seaboard, and the lodgment gained by the brilliant naval victories at Hatteras and Port Royal, already presaged the fate of disunion. In a rough and hasty measurement of strength and unity, political and military, the relative proportions of population, wealth, and skill, and the no less potent elements of devotion to freedom, justice, and humanity, had already so far turned the scale as to foreshadow, with unerring certainty, that the seceding States would ultimately fail in their desperate appeal from the ballot to the bullet. For the present, however, both the contestants remained confident, determined, and unceasingly active in gathering the huge armies destined, in the coming spring, to renew the mighty conflict.

END.

APPENDIX A.

BRIGADIER-GENERAL IRVIN McDOWELL COMMANDING.

STAFF.

CAPTAIN JAMES B. FRY, Assistant Adjutant-General.
MAJOR W. H. WOOD, 17th Infantry, Acting Inspector-General.
CAPTAIN O. H. TILLINGHAST, Assistant Quartermaster.
CAPTAIN H. F. CLARKE, Chief Commissary of Subsistence.
SURGEON W. S. KING.
ASSISTANT SURGEON D. L. MAGRUDER.
MAJOR J. G. BARNARD, Chief Engineer.
LIEUTENANT FRED. E. PRIME, Engineer.
CAPTAIN A. W. WHIPPLE, Topographical Engineer.
LIEUTENANT H. L. ABBOT, Topographical Engineer.
LIEUTENANT H. S. PUTNAM, Topographical Engineer.
LIEUTENANT GEORGE C. STRONG, Ordnance Officer.
MAJOR A. J. MYER, Signal Officer.
MAJOR WILLIAM F. BARRY, 5th Artillery, Chief of Artillery.
MAJOR JAMES S. WADSWORTH, Volunteer Aid-de-Camp.
MAJOR CLARENCE S. BROWN, Volunteer Aid-de-Camp.
LIEUTENANT H. W. KINGSBURY, 5th Artillery, Aid-de-Camp.
LIEUTENANT GUY V. HENRY, Aid-de-Camp.
MAJOR MALCOLM McDOWELL, Acting Aid-de-Camp.

FIRST DIVISION.

BRIGADIER-GENERAL DANIEL TYLER.

First Brigade.

Colonel ERASMUS D. KEYES.
2d Maine, Colonel Charles D. Jameson.
1st Connecticut, Colonel George S. Burnham.
2d   "   Colonel Alfred H. Terry.
3d   "   Colonel John L. Chatfield.

---

[1] For the complete and correct compilation herewith for the first time printed, the author is indebted to Colonel Robert N. Scott, U. S. A., in charge of the publication of the Official War Records.

Second Brigade.

Brigadier-General ROBERT C. SCHENCK.
2d New York (militia), Colonel George W. B. Tompkins.
1st Ohio, Colonel A. McD. McCook.
2d   "   Lieut.-Colonel Rodney Mason.
Company E, 2d U. S. Artillery, Captain J. H. Carlisle.

Third Brigade.

Colonel WILLIAM T. SHERMAN.
13th New York, Colonel Isaac F. Quinby.
69th   "   Col. Michael Corcoran (wounded and captured), Capt. James Kelly.
79th   "   Colonel James Cameron (killed).
2d Wisconsin, Lieut.-Colonel Henry W. Peck.
Company E, 3d U. S. Artillery, Captain R. B. Ayres.

Fourth Brigade.

Colonel ISRAEL B. RICHARDSON.
1st Massachusetts, Colonel Robert Cowdin.
12th New York, Colonel Ezra L. Walrath.
2d Michigan, Major Adolphus W. Williams.
3d   "   Colonel Daniel McConnell.
Company G, 1st U. S. Artillery, Lieutenant John Edwards.
Company M, 2d U. S. Artillery, Captain Henry J. Hunt.

SECOND DIVISION.

(1.) COLONEL DAVID HUNTER (wounded).
(2.) COLONEL ANDREW PORTER.

First Brigade.

Colonel ANDREW PORTER.
8th New York (militia), Colonel George Lyons.
14th   "   (militia), Colonel Alfred M. Wood (wounded and captured), Lieut.-
    Colonel E. B. Fowler.
27th   "   Colonel H. W. Slocum (wounded), Major J. J. Bartlett.
Battalion U. S. Infantry, Major George Sykes.
Battalion U. S. Marines, Major John G. Reynolds.
Battalion U. S. Cavalry, Major I. N. Palmer.
Company D, 5th U. S. Artillery, Captain Charles Griffin.

Second Brigade.

Colonel AMBROSE E. BURNSIDE.
2d New Hampshire. Col. Gilman Marston (wounded), Lieut.-Col. Frank S. Fiske.
1st Rhode Island, Major Joseph P. Balch.
2d   "   (with battery), Colonel John S. Slocum (killed), Lieut.-Colonel
    Frank Wheaton.
71st New York (with two howitzers), Colonel Henry P. Martin.

THIRD DIVISION.

COLONEL SAMUEL P. HEINTZELMAN (wounded).

First Brigade.

Colonel WILLIAM B. FRANKLIN.
5th Massachusetts, Colonel Samuel C. Lawrence.
11th   "   Colonel George Clark, Jr.
1st Minnesota, Colonel W. A. Gorman.
Company I, 1st U. S. Artillery, Captain James B. Ricketts (wounded and cap-
    tured), Lieutenant Edmund Kirby.

Second Brigade.

Col. ORLANDO B. WILLCOX (wounded and captured), Col. J. H. HOBART WARD.
11th New York, Lieut.-Colonel Noah L. Farnham.
38th   "   Colonel J. H. Hobart Ward, Lieut.-Colonel Addison Farnsworth.
1st Michigan, Major Alonzo F. Bidwell.
4th   "   Colonel Dwight A. Woodbury.
Company D, 2d U. S. Artillery, Captain Richard Arnold.

Third Brigade.

Colonel OLIVER O. HOWARD.
3d Maine, Major Henry G. Staples.
4th   "   Colonel Hiram G. Berry.
5th   "   Colonel Mark H. Dunnell.
2d Vermont, Colonel Henry Whiting.

FOURTH (RESERVE) DIVISION.[1]

BRIGADIER-GENERAL THEODORE RUNYON.

1st New Jersey,[2] Colonel A. J. Johnson.
2d [2]   "   Colonel Henry M. Baker.
3d [2]   "   Colonel William Napton.
4th [2]   "   Colonel Matthew Miller, Jr.
1st [3]   "   Colonel William R. Montgomery.
2d [3]   "   Colonel George W. McLean.
3d [3]   "   Colonel George W. Taylor.
41st New York,[3] Colonel Leopold von Gilsa.

FIFTH DIVISION.[4]

COLONEL DIXON S. MILES.

First Brigade.

Colonel LOUIS BLENKER.
8th New York (volunteers), Lieut.-Colonel Julius Stahel.
29th   "   Colonel Adolph von Steinwehr.
39th   "   Colonel Frederick G. D'Utassy.
27th Pennsylvania, Colonel Max Einstein.
Company A, 2d U. S. Artillery, Captain John C. Tidball.
Bookwood's New York Battery, Captain Charles Bookwood.

Second Brigade.

Colonel THOMAS A. DAVIES.
16th New York, Lieut.-Colonel Samuel Marsh.
18th   "   Colonel William A. Jackson.
31st   "   Colonel Calvin E. Pratt.
32d   "   Colonel Roderic Matheson.
Company G, 2d U. S. Artillery, Lieutenant Oliver D. Greene.

---

[1] Not engaged.
[2] Three months' militia.
[3] Three years' volunteers.
[4] In reserve at Centreville and not engaged in the battle proper. Had some skirmishing with the enemy during the day and while covering the retreat of the army.

APPENDIX B.

Organization, at the dates indicated, of the Confederate Forces Combined at the Battle of Manassas, under the Command of Brigadier-General Johnston, C. S. Army.

ARMY OF THE POTOMAC (AFTERWARDS FIRST CORPS), July 21, 1861.[1]

Brigadier-General G. T. BEAUREGARD.

INFANTRY.

First Brigade.

Brigadier-General M. L. Bonham.
  11th North Carolina.
  2d South Carolina.
  3d " "
  7th " "
  8th " "

Second Brigade.

Brigadier-General R. S. Ewell.
  5th Alabama.
  6th "
  6th Louisiana.

Third Brigade.

Brigadier-General D. R. Jones.
  17th Mississippi.
  18th "
  5th South Carolina.

Fourth Brigade.

Brigadier-General J. Longstreet.
  5th North Carolina.
  1st Virginia.
  11th "
  17th "

Fifth Brigade.

Colonel P. St. George Cocke.
  1st Louisiana Battalion.
  8th Virginia, seven companies.
  18th "
  19th "
  28th "
  49th "   three companies.

Sixth Brigade.

Colonel J. A. Early.
  13th Mississippi.
  4th South Carolina.
  7th Virginia.
  24th "

Holmes's Reserve Brigade.

Brigadier-General T. H. Holmes.
  2d Tennessee.
  1st Arkansas.
  Walker's Battery.

---

[1] From a field return for that date, but dated September 25, 1861. The reports following show other combinations during the battle.

Troops not brigaded.

7th Louisiana Infantry.
8th   "   "
Hampton Legion (South Carolina) Infantry.
30th Virginia Cavalry.
Harrison's Battalion Cavalry.
Independent Companies (ten) Cavalry.
Washington (Louisiana) Battalion Artillery.

ARTILLERY.

Kemper's Battery.   Loudoun Battery.
Latham's Battery.   Shields's Battery.
              Camp Pickens Companies.

ARMY OF THE SHENANDOAH (JOHNSTON'S DIVISION), JUNE 30, 1861.[1]

BRIGADIER-GENERAL JOSEPH E. JOHNSTON.

First Brigade.

Colonel T. J. JACKSON.
2d Virginia Infantry.
4th   "   "
5th   "   "
27th   "   "
Pendleton's Battery.

Second Brigade.

Colonel F. S. BARTOW.
7th Georgia Infantry.
8th   "   "
9th   "   "
Duncan's Kentucky Battalion.
Pope's Kentucky Battalion.
Alburtis's Battery.

Third Brigade.

Brigadier-General B. E. BEE.
4th Alabama Infantry.
2d Mississippi   "
11th   "   "
1st Tennessee   "
Imboden's Battery.

Fourth Brigade.

Colonel A. ELZEY.
1st Maryland (Battalion) Infantry.
3d Tennessee Infantry.
10th Virginia   "
13th   "   "
Grove's Battery.

Not brigaded.
1st Virginia Cavalry.
33d   "   Infantry.

---

[1] From return of that date.

INDEX.